PRENTICE HALL

CONCEPTUAL PHYSICS
The High School Physics Program

Concept-Development
Practice Book

Paul G. Hewitt

PEARSON

Boston, Massachusetts
Glenview, Illinois
Shoreview, Minnesota
Upper Saddle River, New Jersey

13-digit ISBN 978-0-13-364730-3

10-digit ISBN 0-13-364730-7

 16 18

Contents

To the Student

We all like to enjoy ourselves. One of the things we enjoy is discovering we can do things that we thought we couldn't, like throwing a ball farther than we thought we could, or performing an acrobatic feat we thought only other people could do. It's also fun to get the best from our brains—to discover we can comprehend concepts and ideas we thought we couldn't. This book of practice pages will help you to understand the concepts of physics.

These practice pages are to *teach* you—not to *test* you. Use your textbook with these pages and consult with classmates when you need help—or when they need help. Your teacher will probably not grade these, but will instead base your grade on test scores (that will indirectly relate to how well you do with these practice pages). So these pages are to help you get the hang of physics—something you will likely find enjoyable and worthwhile.

To the Teacher

These are *concept-development* practice pages and are designed for the second stage of the learning cycle. As such, they should *follow* classroom discussion of chapter material. Whether used by students in small groups, in pairs, or even solo, these pages help your students "tie it all together." Your students will not only learn from these, but find that learning physics can be an enjoyable activity—especially if the practice pages are non-threatening. Since the purpose of this book is to teach, rather than test, it is strongly advised not to grade students on this stage of their learning. Ample test material is provided in the test bank supplement.

Some of these pages are easy for many students and some are challenging. In every case, the topics are central to *Conceptual Physics*. So for those who find a particular concept easy to grasp, hooray! And for those who need more help, practice pages serve as a tutor.

So this book is your teaching tool. Whether used as a required stage of learning or an optional one, the choice is yours. But please *do* use, and you'll all enjoy!

Dedicated to

**Students who wonder
and
Their teachers who instill a love of science**

Making Hypotheses

The word *science* comes from Latin, meaning "to know." The word *hypothesis* comes from Greek, "under an idea." A hypothesis (an educated guess) often leads to new knowledge and may help to establish a theory.

WHICH IS AN EDUCATED GUESS---
A HYPOTHESIS OR A THEORY?

WHICH RESULTS FROM A LARGE BODY OF KNOWLEDGE?

Examples:

1. We see items in a store priced at $2.98, $3.98, or $4.98 etc. Why not $3, $4, or $5, etc? Make a hypothesis for this by finishing the following:

    Items in a store are usually priced one or two cents lower than the nearest dollar because

    _____

    _____

    _____

    _____

    Suggest a way to test this hypothesis. (*Hint:* Imagine you own a chain of stores.)

    _____

    _____

    _____

    _____

Another hypothesis is based on distrust of sales clerks before the use of cash registers. In those days, money was handled only by store owners. A customer buying a $5 item would give a $5 bill to the clerk who might "forget" to give it to the store owner at the cashier's window. At $4.98 the customer wants the change (2 cents), and so the clerk must go to the store owner to get it. Thus tradition and a custom started. How could you support the hypothesis that store owners established pricing policies to protect themselves against sales clerks? (*Hint:* Imagine you have a librarian friend who has information on F.W. Woolworth.)

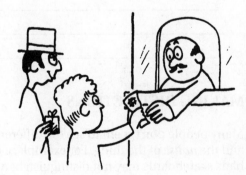

_____

_____

_____

CONCEPTUAL PHYSICS

2. It is well known that things generally expand when heated. An iron plate gets slightly bigger, for example, when put in a hot oven. But what of a hole in the middle of the iron? Will the hole get bigger or smaller when expansion occurs? One friend says the size of the hole will increase, and another says it will decrease.

a. What is your hypothesis about hole size, and if you are wrong, is there a test for finding out?

_____

_____

_____

b. There are often several ways to test a hypothesis. For example, you can perform a physical experiment and witness the results yourself, or you can use the library to find the reported results of other investigators. Which of these two methods do you favor, and why?

_____

_____

3. Before the time of the printing press, books were hand-copied by scribes, many of whom were monks in monasteries. There is the story of the scribe who was frustrated to find a smudge on an important page he was copying. The smudge blotted out part of the sentence that reported the number of teeth in the head of a donkey. The scribe was very upset and didn't know what to do. He consulted with other scribes to see if any of their books stated the number of teeth in the head of a donkey. After many hours of fruitless searching through the library, it was agreed that the best thing to do was to send a messenger by donkey to the next monastery and continue the search there. What would be your advice?

_____

_____

MAKING DISTINCTIONS

Many people don't seem to see the difference between a thing and the *abuse* of the thing. For example, a city council that bans skateboards may not distinguish between skateboarding and reckless skateboarding. A person who advocates that technology be banned may not distinguish between technology and the abuses of technology. There is a difference between a thing and the abuse of the thing. On a separate sheet of paper, list examples you can think of—then discuss your list and those of others with classmates.

CONCEPTUAL PHYSICS

Static Equilibrium

1. Little Nellie Newton wishes to be a gymnast and hangs from a variety of positions as shown. Since she is not accelerating, the net force on her is zero. That is, $\sum F = 0$. This means the upward pull of the rope(s) equals the downward pull of gravity. She weighs 300 N. Show the scale reading(s) for each case.

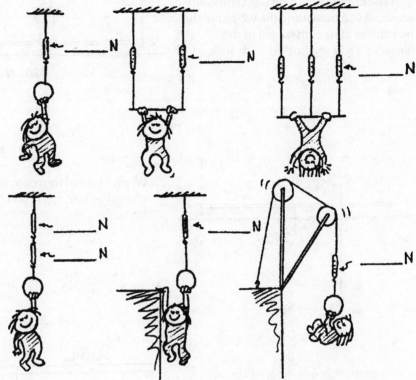

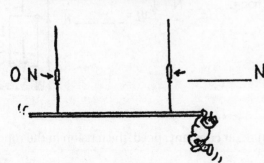

2. When Burl the painter stands in the exact middle of his staging, the left scale reads 600 N. Fill in the reading on the right scale. The total weight of Burl and staging must be

   _____ N.

3. Burl stands farther from the left. Fill in the reading on the right scale.

4. In a silly mood, Burl dangles from the right end. Fill in the reading on the right scale.

CONCEPTUAL PHYSICS

The Equilibrium Rule: ΣF = 0

1. Manuel weighs 1000 N and stands in the middle of a board that weighs 200 N. The ends of the board rest on bathroom scales. (We can assume the weight of the board acts at its center.) Fill in the correct weight reading on each scale.

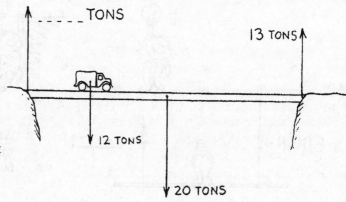

2. When Manuel moves to the left as shown, the scale closest to him reads 850 N. Fill in the weight for the far scale.

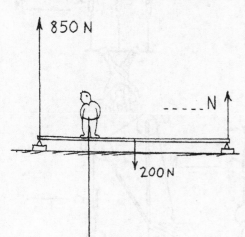

3. A 12-ton truck is one-quarter the way across a bridge that weighs 20 tons. A 13-ton force supports the right side of the bridge as shown. How much support force is on the left side?

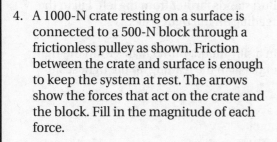

4. A 1000-N crate resting on a surface is connected to a 500-N block through a frictionless pulley as shown. Friction between the crate and surface is enough to keep the system at rest. The arrows show the forces that act on the crate and the block. Fill in the magnitude of each force.

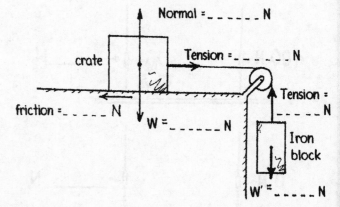

5. If the crate and block in the preceding question move at constant speed, the tension in the rope (is the same) (increases) (decreases).
   The sliding system is then in (static equilibrium) (dynamic equilibrium).

Vectors and Equilibrium

1. Nellie Newton dangles
   from a vertical rope
   in equilibrium: $\sum F = 0$.
   The tension in the rope
   (upward vector) has the same
   magnitude as the downward
   pull of gravity (downward vector).

2. Nellie is supported by
   two vertical ropes.
   Draw tension vectors
   to scale along the direction
   of each rope.

3. This time the vertical ropes
   have different lengths. Draw
   tension vectors to scale for
   each of the two ropes.

4. Nellie is supported by three
   vertical ropes that are
   equally taut but have
   different lengths. Again,
   draw tension vectors to scale
   for each of the three ropes.

Circle the correct answers.

5. We see that tension in a rope is (dependent on)　(independent of)　the length of the rope. So the length

   of a vector representing rope tension is (dependent on)　(independent of)　the length of the rope.

CONCEPTUAL PHYSICS

Fill in the magnitudes of net force for each case.

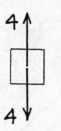

$F_{net} =$ _____

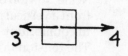

$F_{net} =$ _____

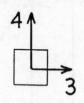

$F_{net} =$ _____

$F_{net} =$ _____

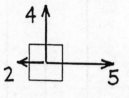

$F_{net} =$ _____

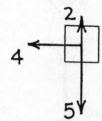

$F_{net} =$ _____

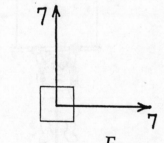

$F_{net} =$ _____

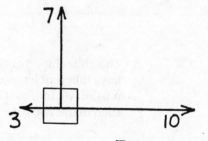

$F_{net} =$ _____

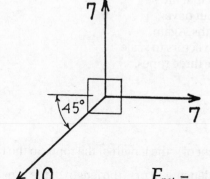

$F_{net} =$ _____

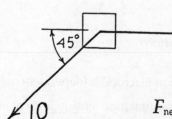

$F_{net} =$ _____

CONCEPTUAL PHYSICS

Vectors and Equilibrium

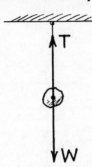

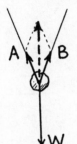

The rock hangs at rest from a single string. Only two forces act on it, the upward tension **T** of the string, and the downward pull of gravity **W**. The forces are equal in magnitude and opposite in direction.

Net force on the rock is (zero) (greater than zero).

Here the rock is suspended by 2 strings. Tension in each string acts in a direction along the string. We'll show tension of the left string by vector **A**, and tension of the right string by vector **B**. The resultant of **A** and **B** is found by the **parallelogram rule**, and is shown by the dashed vector. Note it has the same magnitude as **W**, so the net force on the rock is

(zero) (greater than zero).

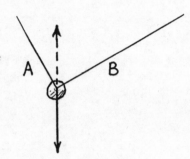

Consider strings at unequal angles. The resultant **A + B** is still equal and opposite to **W**, and is shown by the dashed vector. Construct the appropriate parallelogram to produce this resultant. Show the relative magnitudes of **A** and **B**.

Tension in **A** is (less than) (equal to) (greater than) tension in **B**.

Repeat the procedure for the arrangement below.

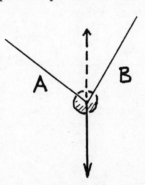

Here tension is greater in _____.

No wonder hanging from a horizontal tightly-stretched clothesline breaks it!

Construct vectors **A** and **B** for the cases below. First draw a vector **W**, then the parallelogram that has equal and opposite vector **A + B** as the diagonal. Then find approximate magnitudes of **A** and **B**.

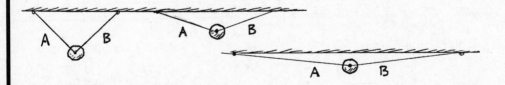

CONCEPTUAL PHYSICS

**Concept-Development
Practice Page**

3-1

Mass and Weight

Learning physics is learning the connections among concepts in nature, and
also learning to distinguish between closely related concepts. Velocity and
acceleration, which are treated in the next chapter, are often confused. Similarly
in this chapter, we find that mass and weight are often confused. They aren't the
same! Please review the distinction between mass and weight in your textbook. To
reinforce your understanding of this distinction, circle the correct answers below.

Comparing the concepts of mass and weight, one is basic—fundamental—
depending only on the internal makeup of an object and the number and kind of atoms that compose
it. The concept that is fundamental is (mass) (weight).

The concept that additionally depends on location in a gravitational field is (mass) (weight).

(Mass) (Weight) is a measure of the amount of matter in an object and only depends on
the number and kind of atoms that compose it.

It can correctly be said that (mass) (weight) is a measure of "laziness" of an object.

(Mass) (Weight) is related to the gravitational force acting on the object.

(Mass) (Weight) depends on an object's location, whereas (mass) (weight) does not.

In other words, a stone would have the same (mass) (weight) whether it is on the surface of Earth or on
the surface of the moon. However, its (mass) (weight) depends on its location.

On the moon's surface, where gravity is only about one sixth of Earth gravity (mass) (weight)
(both the mass and the weight) of the stone would be the same as on Earth.

While mass and weight are not the same, they are (directly proportional) (inversely proportional)
to each other. In the same location, twice the mass has (twice) (half) the weight.

The International System of Units (SI) unit of mass is the (kilogram) (newton), and the SI unit of
force is the (kilogram) (newton).

In the United States, it is common to measure the mass of something by measuring its gravitational pull
to Earth, its weight. The common unit of weight in the U.S. is the (pound) (kilogram) (newton).

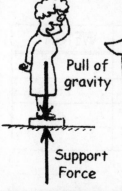

Pull of
gravity

Support
Force

When I step on a weighing scale, two forces act on it; a downward
pull of gravity, and an upward support force. These equal and
opposite forces effectively compress a spring inside the scale that
is calibrated to show weight. When in equilibrium, my weight = *mg*.

CONCEPTUAL PHYSICS

Converting Mass to Weight

Objects with mass also have weight (although they can be weightless under special conditions). If you know the mass of something in **kilograms** and want its weight in **newtons**, at Earth's surface, you can take advantage of the formula that relates weight and mass.

Weight = mass × acceleration due to gravity
$W = mg$

This is in accord with Newton's second law, written as $F = ma$. When the force of gravity is the only force, the acceleration of any object of mass m will be g, the acceleration of free fall. Importantly, g acts as a proportionality constant, 10 N/kg, which is equivalent to 10 m/s².

Sample Question:
How much does a 1-kg bag of nails weigh on Earth?

$W = mg = (1 \text{ kg})(10 \text{ m/s}^2) = 10 \text{ kg} \cdot \text{m/s}^2 = 10 \text{ N}$,
or simply, $W = mg = (1 \text{ kg})(10 \text{ N/kg}) = 10 \text{ N}$.

> From $F = ma$, we see that the unit of force equals the units [kg × m/s²]. Can you see the units [m/s²] = [N/kg]?

Answer the following questions.
Felicia the ballet dancer has a mass of 45.0 kg.

1. What is Felicia's weight in newtons at Earth's surface? _____

2. Given that 1 kilogram of mass corresponds to 2.2 pounds at Earth's surface, what is Felicia's weight in pounds on Earth? _____

3. What would be Felicia's mass on the surface of Jupiter? _____

4. What would be Felicia's weight on Jupiter's surface, where the acceleration due to gravity is 25.0 m/s²? _____

Different masses are hung on a spring scale calibrated in newtons. The force exerted by gravity on 1 kg = 10 N.

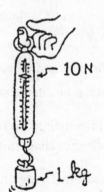

5. The force exerted by gravity on 5 kg = _____ N.

6. The force exerted by gravity on _____ kg = 100 N.

Make up your own mass and show the corresponding weight:
The force exerted by gravity on _____ kg = _____ N.

By whatever means (spring scales, measuring balances, etc.), find the mass of your physics book. Then complete the table.

OBJECT	MASS	WEIGHT
MELON	1 kg	
APPLE		1 N
BOOK		
A FRIEND	60 kg	

CONCEPTUAL PHYSICS

Concept-Development Practice Page **3-2**

Inertia

Circle the correct answers.

1. An astronaut in outer space away from gravitational or frictional forces throws a rock. The rock will

   (gradually slow to a stop)

   (continue moving in a straight line at constant speed).

   The rock's tendency to do this is called

   (inertia) (weight) (acceleration).

2.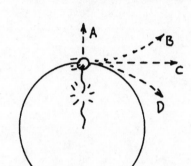

   The sketch shows a top view of a rock being whirled at the end of a string (clockwise). If the string breaks, the path of the rock is

   (A) (B) (C) (D).

3. Suppose you are standing in the aisle of a bus that travels along a straight road at 100 km/h, and you hold a pencil still above your head. Then relative to the bus, the velocity of the pencil is 0 km/h, and relative to the road, the pencil has a horizontal velocity of

   (less than 100 km/h) (100 km/h) (more than 100 km/h).

   Suppose you release the pencil. While it is dropping, and relative to the road, the pencil still has a horizontal velocity of

   (less than 100 km/h) (100 km/h) (more than 100 km/h).

   This means that the pencil will strike the floor at a place directly

   (behind you) (at your feet below your hand) (in front of you).

   Relative to you, the way the pencil drops

   (is the same as if the bus were at rest)

   (depends on the velocity of the bus).

   How does this example illustrate the law of inertia?

   _____

   _____

   _____

CONCEPTUAL PHYSICS

**Concept-Development
Practice Page** | 4-1

Free Fall Speed

1. Aunt Minnie gives you $10 per second for 4 seconds. How much money do you have after 4 seconds? _____

2. A ball dropped from rest picks up speed at 10 m per second. After it falls for 4 seconds, how fast is it going? _____

3. You have $20, and Uncle Harry gives you $10 each second for 3 seconds. How much money do you have after 3 seconds? _____

4. A ball is thrown straight down with an initial speed of 20 m/s. After 3 seconds, how fast is it going? _____

5. You have $50 and you pay Aunt Minnie $10/second. When will your money run out? _____

6. You shoot an arrow straight up at 50 m/s. When will it run out of speed? _____

7. So what will be the arrow's speed 5 seconds after you shoot it? _____

8. What will its speed be 6 seconds after you shoot it? 7 seconds? _____

Free Fall Distance

1. Speed is one thing; distance another. *Where* is the arrow you shoot up at 50 m/s when it runs out of speed? _____

2. How high will the arrow be 7 seconds after being shot up at 50 m/s? _____

3. a. Aunt Minnie drops a penny into a wishing well and and it falls for 3 seconds before hitting the water. How fast is it going when it hits? _____

   b. What is the penny's average speed during its 3-second drop? _____

   c. How far down is the water surface? _____

FROM REST,
$v = 10t$
$d = 5t^2$

4. Aunt Minnie didn't get her wish, so she goes to a deeper wishing well and throws a penny straight down into it at 10 m/s. How far does this penny go in 3 seconds? _____

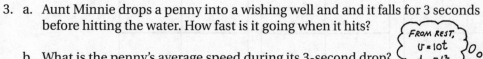

$$\bar{v} = \frac{v_i + v}{2} = \frac{v_o + 10t}{2}$$
THEN $d = \bar{v}t$

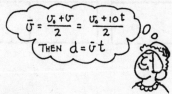

Distinguish between "how fast," "how far," and "how long"!

CONCEPTUAL PHYSICS

Straight Up and Down

The sketch is similar to Figure 4.9 in the textbook.
Assume negligible air resistance and $g = 10$ m/s^2.

- Table 1 shows the velocity data of the figure for $t = 0$ to $t = 8$ seconds.
  Complete the table.
  Distances traveled are from the starting point (the *displacements*).

- Table 2 is for a greater initial velocity. Complete it.

- Table 3 doesn't specify an initial velocity. Choose your own
  and complete the table accordingly.

Choosing up as +, down as −,
$v = v_o - gt$
then falling from rest when $v_o = 0$,
$v = -gt$
or $v = -(10\tfrac{m}{s})t$

With initial velocity v_o;
$d = v_o t - \tfrac{1}{2}gt^2$ or $d = v_o t - (5\tfrac{m}{s})t^2$
Falling from rest when $v_o = 0$,
$d = -(5\tfrac{m}{s})t^2$

3 s   velocity = 0

2 s   4 s
$v = 10$ m/s $v = -10$ m/s

1 s   5 s
$v = 20$ m/s $v = -20$ m/s

0 s   6 s
$v = 30$ m/s $v = -30$ m/s

7 s
$v = -40$ m/s

Notice g is constant;
velocity changes by
−10 m/s each second!

Time in seconds	1. Velocity m/s	Distance m	2. Velocity m/s	Distance m	3. Velocity m/s	Distance m
0	30	0	40	0		0
1	20					
2	10					
3	0					
4	−10					
5	−20					
6	−30					
7	−40					
8	−50					

CONCEPTUAL PHYSICS

Free Fall

1. A rock dropped from the top of a cliff picks up speed as it falls. Pretend that a speedometer and odometer are attached to the rock to show readings of speed and distance at 1-second intervals. Both speed and distance are zero at time = zero (see sketch). Note that after falling 1 second, the speed reading is 10 m/s and the distance fallen is 5 m. The readings for succeeding seconds of fall are not shown and are left for you to complete. Draw the position of the speedometer pointer and write in the correct odometer reading for each time. Use $g = 10 \text{ m/s}^2$ and neglect air resistance.

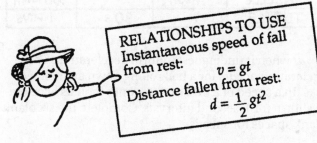

RELATIONSHIPS TO USE
Instantaneous speed of fall from rest:
$$v = gt$$
Distance fallen from rest:
$$d = \frac{1}{2}gt^2$$

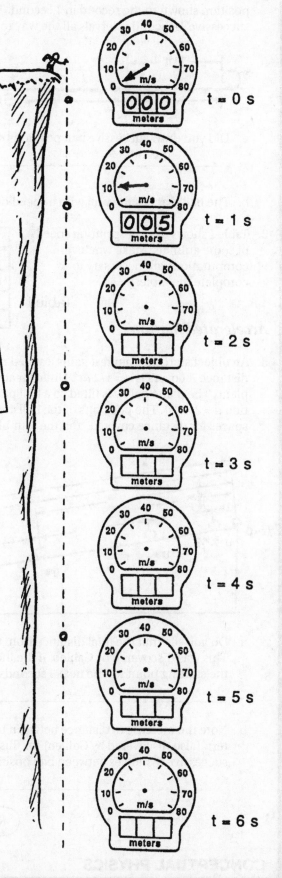

t = 0 s

t = 1 s

t = 2 s

t = 3 s

t = 4 s

t = 5 s

t = 6 s

a. The speedometer reading increased by the same amount, _____ m/s, each second. This increase in speed per second is called _____.

b. The distance fallen increases as the square of the _____.

c. If it takes 7 seconds to reach the ground, then its speed at impact is _____ m/s, the total distance fallen is _____ m, and its acceleration of fall just before impact is _____ m/s².

CONCEPTUAL PHYSICS

Non-Accelerated Motion

1. The sketch shows a ball rolling at constant velocity along a level floor. The ball rolls from the first position shown to the second in 1 second. The two positions are 1 meter apart. Sketch the ball at successive 1-second intervals all the way to the wall (neglect resistance).

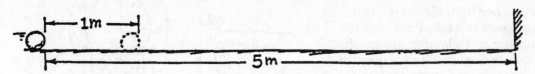

   a. Did you draw successive ball positions evenly spaced, farther apart, or closer together? Why?

   _____

   b. The ball reaches the wall with a speed of _____ m/s and takes a time of _____ seconds.

2. Table I shows data of sprinting speeds of some animals. Make whatever computations are necessary to complete the table.

   Table I

ANIMAL	DISTANCE	TIME	SPEED
CHEETAH	75 m	3 s	25 m/s
GREYHOUND	160 m	10 s	
GAZELLE	1 km		100 km/h
TURTLE		30 s	1 cm/s

Accelerated Motion

3. An object starting from rest gains a speed $v = at$ when it undergoes uniform acceleration. The distance it covers is $d = 1/2\ at^2$. Uniform acceleration occurs for a ball rolling down an inclined plane. The plane below is tilted so a ball picks up a speed of 2 m/s each second; then its acceleration $a = 2\ \text{m/s}^2$. The positions of the ball are shown for 1-second intervals. Complete the six blank spaces for distance covered, and the four blank spaces for speeds.

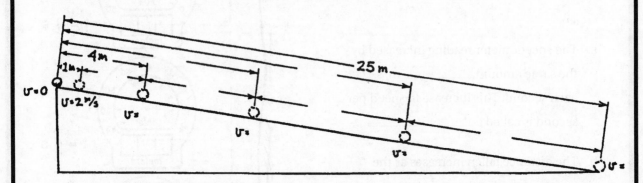

   a. Do you see that the total distance from the starting point increases as the square of the time? This was discovered by Galileo. If the incline were to continue, predict the ball's distance from the starting point for the next 3 seconds.

   _____

   b. Note the increase of distance between ball positions with time. Do you see an odd-integer pattern (also discovered by Galileo) for this increase? If the incline were to continue, predict the successive distances between ball positions for the next 3 seconds.

   _____

   Now you're ready for "Merrily We Roll Along!" in the lab manual!

CONCEPTUAL PHYSICS

Hang Time

Some athletes and dancers have great jumping ability. When leaping, they seem to momentarily "hang in the air" and defy gravity. The time that a jumper is airborne with feet off the ground is called hang time. Ask your friends to estimate the hang time of the great jumpers. They may say two or three seconds. But surprisingly, the hang time of the greatest jumpers is most always less than 1 second! A longer time is one of many illusions we have about nature.

To better understand this, find the answers to the following questions:

1. If you step off a table and it takes one-half second to reach the floor, what will be the speed when you meet the floor?

_____

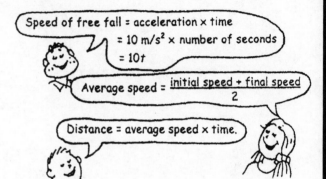

Speed of free fall = acceleration × time
= 10 m/s² × number of seconds
= 10t

Average speed = $\dfrac{\text{initial speed + final speed}}{2}$

Distance = average speed × time.

2. What will be your average speed of fall?

_____

3. What will be the distance of fall?

_____

4. So how high is the surface of the table above the floor? _____

Jumping ability is best measured by a standing vertical jump. Stand facing a wall with feet flat on the floor and arms extended upward. Make a mark on the wall at the top of your reach. Then make your jump, and at the peak make another mark. The distance between these two marks measures your vertical leap. If it's more than 0.6 meters (2 feet), you're exceptional.

5. What is your vertical jumping distance? _____

6. Calculate your personal hang time using the formula $d = 1/2\ gt^2$. (Remember that hang time is the time that you move upward + the time you return downward.)

Almost anybody can safely step off a 1.25-m (4-feet) high table. Can anybody in your school jump from the floor up onto the same table?

No way!

There's a big difference in how high you can reach and how high you raise your "center of gravity" when you jump. Even basketball star Michael Jordan in his prime couldn't quite raise his body 1.25 meters high, although he could easily reach higher than the more-than-3-meter high basket.

Here we're talking about vertical motion. How about running jumps? We'll see in Chapter 5 that the height of a jump depends only on the jumper's vertical speed at launch. While airborne, the jumper's horizontal speed remains constant while the vertical speed undergoes acceleration due to gravity. While airborne, no amount of leg or arm pumping or other bodily motions can change your hang time.

CONCEPTUAL PHYSICS

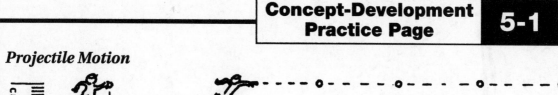

Concept-Development Practice Page **5-1**

Projectile Motion

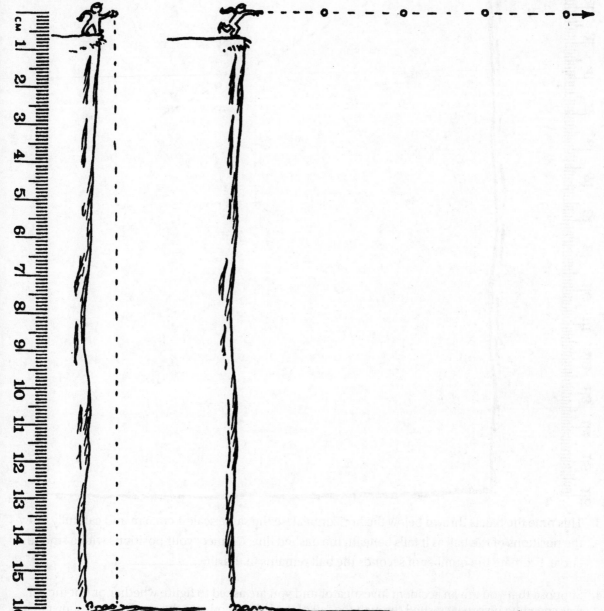

1. Above left: Use the scale 1 cm:5 m and draw the positions of the dropped ball at 1-second intervals. Neglect air drag and assume $g = 10$ m/s^2. Estimate the number of seconds the ball is in the air.

   _____ seconds

2. Above right: The four positions of the thrown ball with *no gravity* are at 1-second intervals. At 1 cm:5 m, carefully draw the positions of the ball *with* gravity. Neglect air drag and assume $g = 10$ m/s^2. Connect your positions with a smooth curve to show the path of the ball. How is the motion in the vertical direction affected by motion in the horizontal direction?

   _____

CONCEPTUAL PHYSICS

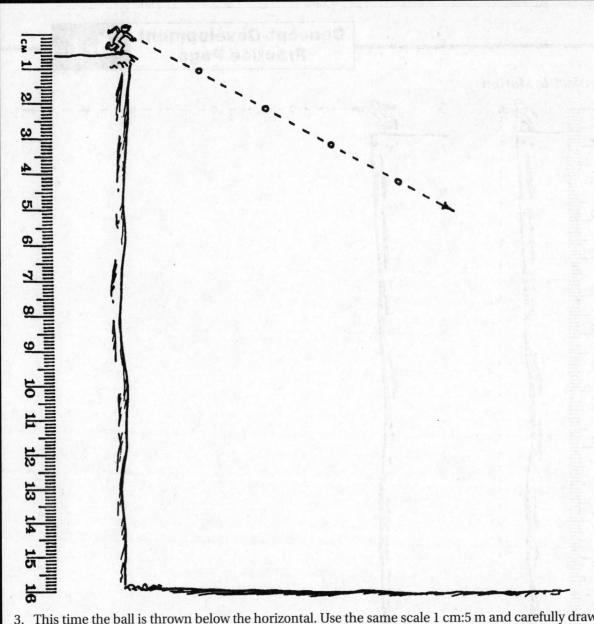

3. This time the ball is thrown below the horizontal. Use the same scale 1 cm:5 m and carefully draw the positions of the ball as it falls beneath the dashed line. Connect your positions with a smooth curve. Estimate the number of seconds the ball remains in the air. _____ s

4. Suppose that you are an accident investigator and you are asked to figure whether or not the car was speeding before it crashed through the rail of the bridge and into the mudbank as shown. The speed limit on the bridge is 55 mph = 24 m/s. What is your conclusion?

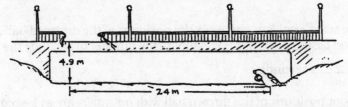

_____

_____

_____

_____

CONCEPTUAL PHYSICS

Concept-Development Practice Page | 5-2

Vectors

Use the parallelogram rule to carefully construct the resultants for the eight pairs of vectors.

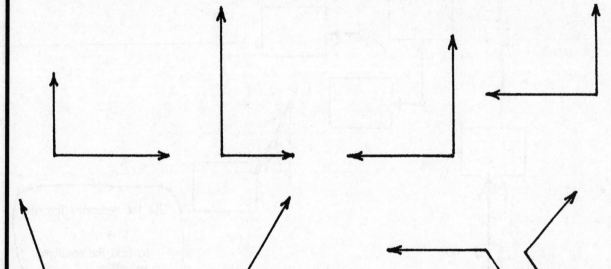

Carefully construct the vertical and horizontal components of the eight vectors.

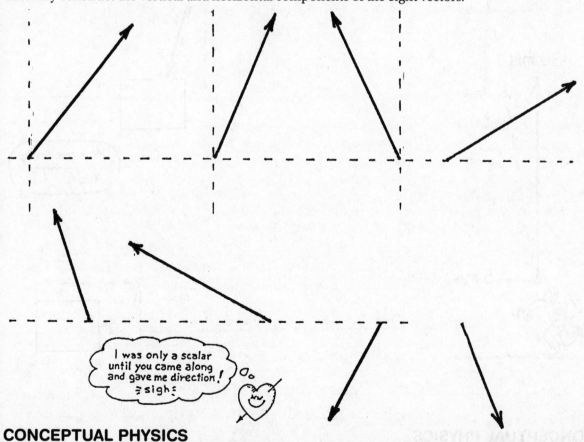

CONCEPTUAL PHYSICS

Tossed Ball

A ball tossed upward has initial velocity components 30 m/s vertical, and 5 m/s horizontal. The position of the ball is shown at 1-second intervals. Air resistance is negligible, and $g = 10$ m/s^2. Fill in the boxes, writing in the values of velocity *components* ascending, and your calculated *resultant velocities* descending.

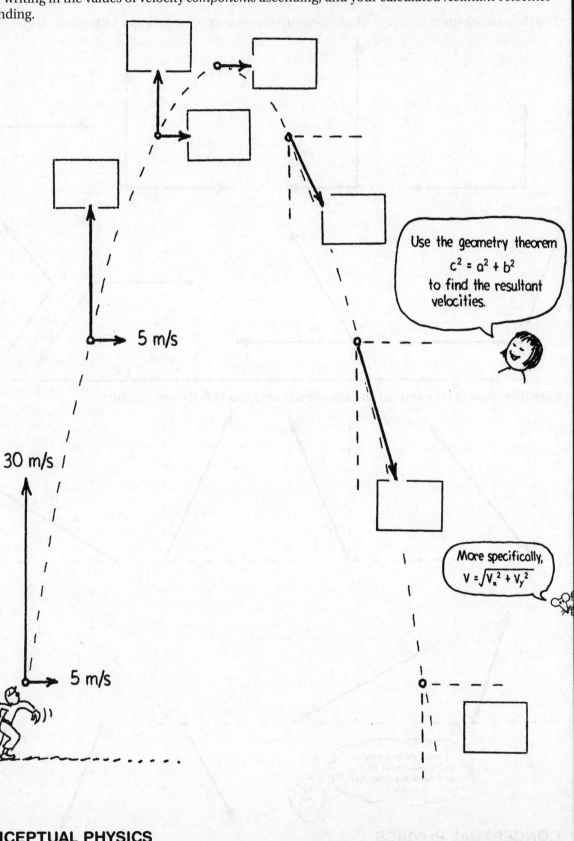

Vectors and the Parallelogram Rule

1. When two vectors **A** and **B** are at an angle to each other, they add to produce the resultant **C** by the *parallelogram rule*. Note that **C** is the diagonal of a parallelogram where **A** and **B** are adjacent sides. Resultant **C** is shown in the first two diagrams, (a) and (b). Construct resultant **C** in diagrams (c) and (d). Note that in diagram (d) you form a rectangle (a special case of a parallelogram).

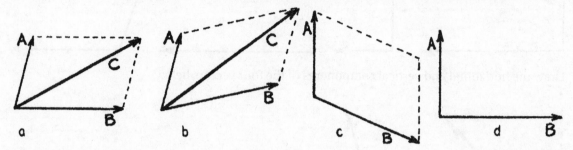

2. Below we see a top view of an airplane being blown off course by wind in various directions. Use the parallelogram rule to show the resulting speed and direction of travel for each case. In which case does the airplane travel fastest across the ground? _____ Slowest? _____

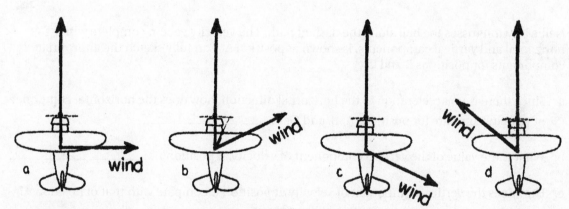

3. To the right we see the top views of 3 motorboats crossing a river. All have the same speed relative to the water, and all experience the same water flow.

Construct resultant vectors showing the speed and direction of the boats.

a. Which boat takes the shortest path to the opposite shore?

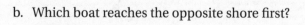

b. Which boat reaches the opposite shore first?

_____

c. Which boat provides the fastest ride?

_____

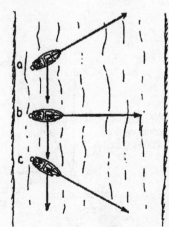

CONCEPTUAL PHYSICS

Velocity Vectors and Components

1. Draw the resultants of the four sets of vectors below.

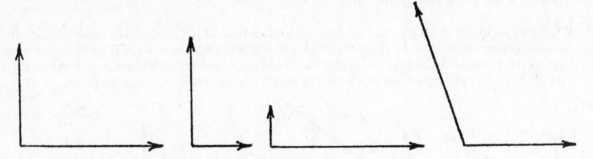

2. Draw the horizontal and vertical components of the four vectors below.

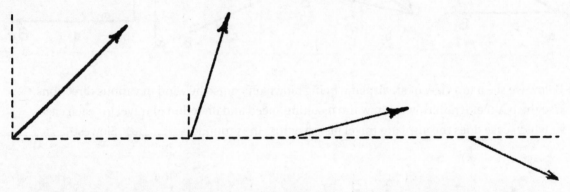

3. Nellie Newton tosses the ball along the dashed path. The velocity vector, complete with its horizontal and vertical components, is shown at position A. Carefully sketch the appropriate components for positions B and C.

   a. Since there is no acceleration in the horizontal direction, how does the horizontal component of velocity compare for positions A, B, and C? _____

   b. What is the value of the vertical component of velocity at position B? _____

   c. How does the vertical component of velocity at position C compare with that of position A?

   _____

   _____

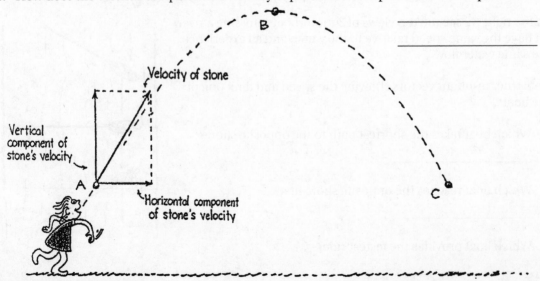

Velocity of stone

Vertical component of stone's velocity

Horizontal component of stone's velocity

CONCEPTUAL PHYSICS

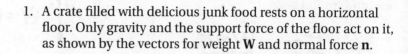

Concept-Development Practice Page

6-1

Friction

1. A crate filled with delicious junk food rests on a horizontal floor. Only gravity and the support force of the floor act on it, as shown by the vectors for weight **W** and normal force **n**.

   a. The net force on the crate is (zero) (greater than zero).

   b. Evidence for this is _____.

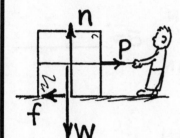

2. A slight pull **P** is exerted on the crate, not enough to move it.

   a. The force of friction **f** acting on the crate is

      (less than) (equal to) (greater than) **P**.

   b. The net force on the crate is (zero) (greater than zero).

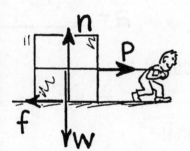

3. Pull **P** is increased until the crate begins to move. It is pulled so that it moves with constant velocity across the floor.

   a. Friction **f** is (less than) (equal to) (greater than) **P**.

   b. Constant velocity means acceleration is

      (zero) (greater than zero).

   c. The net force on the crate is (less than) (equal to) (greater than) zero.

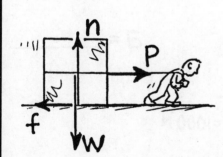

4. Pull **P** is further increased and is now greater than friction **f**.

   a. The net force on the crate is (less than) (equal to) (greater than) zero.

   b. The net force acts toward the right, so acceleration acts toward the (left) (right).

5. If the pulling force **P** is 150 N and the crate doesn't move, what is the magnitude of **f**? _____

6. If the pulling force **P** is 200 N and the crate doesn't move, what is the magnitude of **f**? _____

7. If the force of sliding friction is 250 N, what force is necessary to keep the crate sliding at constant velocity? _____

8. If the mass of the crate is 50 kg and sliding friction is 250 N, what is the acceleration of the crate when the pulling force is 250 N? _____ 300 N? _____ 500 N? _____

CONCEPTUAL PHYSICS

Falling and Air Resistance

Bronco skydives and parachutes from a stationary helicopter. Various stages of fall are shown in positions (a) through (f). Using Newton's second law,

$$a = \frac{F_{NET}}{m} = \frac{W-R}{m}$$

find Bronco's acceleration at each position (answer in the blanks to the right). You need to know that Bronco's mass m is 100 kg so his weight is a constant 1000 N. Air resistance R varies with speed and cross-sectional area as shown.

Circle the correct answers.

1. When Bronco's speed is least, his acceleration is

   (least) (most).

2. In which position(s) does Bronco experience a downward acceleration?

   (a) (b) (c) (d) (e) (f)

3. In which position(s) does Bronco experience an upward acceleration?

   (a) (b) (c) (d) (e) (f)

4. When Bronco experiences an upward acceleration, his velocity is

   (still downward) (upward also).

5. In which position(s) is Bronco's velocity constant?

   (a) (b) (c) (d) (e) (f)

6. In which position(s) does Bronco experience terminal velocity?

   (a) (b) (c) (d) (e) (f)

7. In which position(s) is terminal velocity greatest?

   (a) (b) (c) (d) (e) (f)

8. If Bronco were heavier, his terminal velocity would be

   (greater) (less) (the same).

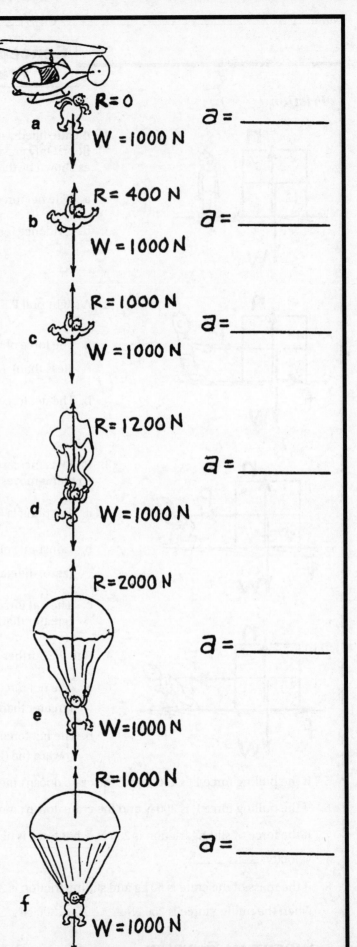

a
R = 0
W = 1000 N
$a =$ _____

b
R = 400 N
W = 1000 N
$a =$ _____

c
R = 1000 N
W = 1000 N
$a =$ _____

d
R = 1200 N
W = 1000 N
$a =$ _____

e
R = 2000 N
W = 1000 N
$a =$ _____

f
R = 1000 N
W = 1000 N
$a =$ _____

CONCEPTUAL PHYSICS

Concept-Development Practice Page | 6-2

Force and Acceleration

1. Skelly the skater, total mass 25 kg, is propelled by rocket power.

   a. Complete Table I
      (neglect resistance)

   TABLE I

FORCE	ACCELERATION
100 N	
200 N	
	10 m/s²

   b. Complete Table II for a
      constant 50-N resistance.

   TABLE II

FORCE	ACCELERATION
50 N	0 m/s²
100 N	
200 N	

2. Block A on a horizontal friction-free table is accelerated by a force from
   a string attached to Block B. B falls vertically and drags A horizontally.
   Both blocks have the same mass m. (Neglect the string's mass.)

   Circle the correct answers.

   a. The *mass* of the system (A + B) is (m) ($2m$).

   b. The *force* that accelerates (A + B) is the weight of (A) (B) (A + B).

   c. The weight of B is ($mg/2$) (mg) ($2mg$).

   d. Acceleration of (A + B) is (less than g) (g) (more than g).

   e. Use $a =$ to show the acceleration of (A + B) as a fraction of g. _____

If B were allowed to fall by itself, not dragging A, then wouldn't its acceleration be g?

Yes, because the force that accelerates it would only be acting on its own mass — not twice the mass!

To better understand this, consider 3 and 4 on the other side!

CONCEPTUAL PHYSICS

3. Suppose A is still a 1-kg block, but B is a low-mass feather (or a coin).

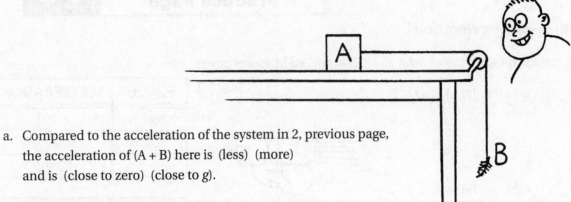

a. Compared to the acceleration of the system in 2, previous page, the acceleration of (A + B) here is (less) (more) and is (close to zero) (close to *g*).

b. In this case the acceleration of B is (practically that of free fall) (constrained).

4. Suppose A is a feather or coin, and B has a mass of 1 kg.

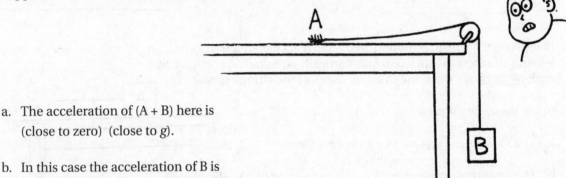

a. The acceleration of (A + B) here is (close to zero) (close to *g*).

b. In this case the acceleration of B is (practically that of free fall) (constrained).

5. Summarizing 2, 3, and 4, where the weight of one object causes the acceleration of two objects, we see the range of possible accelerations is

(between zero and *g*) (between zero and infinity) (between *g* and infinity).

6. A ball rolls down a uniform-slope ramp.

a. Acceleration is (decreasing) (constant) (increasing).

b. If the ramp were steeper, acceleration would be (more) (the same) (less).

c. When the ball reaches the bottom and rolls along the smooth level surface it (continues to accelerate) (does not accelerate).

Now you're ready for the labs " Constant Force and Changing Mass " and " Constant Mass and Changing Force "!

CONCEPTUAL PHYSICS

Racing Day with a = F/m

In each situation below, Cart A has a mass of **1 kg**. *Circle the correct answers* (A, B, or Same for both).

1. Cart A is pulled with a force of **1 N**.
   Cart B also has a mass of **1 kg** and is pulled
   with a force of **2 N**.
   Which undergoes the greater acceleration?

   (A)   (B)   (Same for both)

   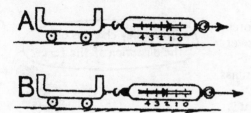

2. Cart A is pulled with a force of **1 N**.
   Cart B has a mass of **2 kg** and is also pulled
   with a force of **1 N**.
   Which undergoes the greater acceleration?

   (A)   (B)   (Same for both)

   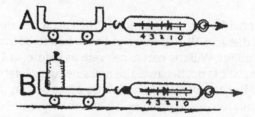

3. Cart A is pulled with a force of **1 N**.
   Cart B has a mass of **2 kg** and is pulled with
   a force of **2 N**.
   Which undergoes the greater acceleration?

   (A)   (B)   (Same for both)

   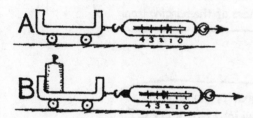

4. Cart A is pulled with a force of **1 N**.
   Cart B has a mass of **3 kg** and is pulled with
   a force of **3 N**.
   Which undergoes the greater acceleration?

   (A)   (B)   (Same for both)

   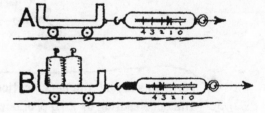

5. This time Cart A is pulled with a force of **4 N**.
   Cart B has a mass of **4 kg** and is pulled with a
   force of **4 N**.
   Which undergoes the greater acceleration?

   (A)   (B)   (Same for both)

   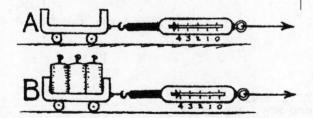

6. Cart A is pulled with a force of **2 N**.
   Cart B has a mass of **4 kg** and is pulled with
   a force of **3 N**.
   Which undergoes the greater acceleration?

   (A)   (B)   (Same for both)

   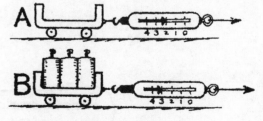

   thanx to Dean Baird

CONCEPTUAL PHYSICS

Drop and Pull

1. Consider a 1-kg cart being pulled by a 10-N applied force. According to Newton's second law, acceleration of the cart is

$$a = \frac{F}{m} = \frac{10\,\text{N}}{1\,\text{kg}} = 10\,\text{m/s}^2.$$

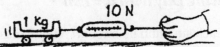

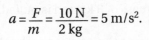
This is the same as the acceleration of free fall, g—because a force equal to the cart's weight accelerates it.

2. Consider the acceleration of the cart when the applied force is due to a 10-N iron weight attached to a string draped over a pulley. Will the cart accelerate as before, at 10 m/s²? The answer is no, because the mass being accelerated is the mass of the cart *plus* the mass of the piece of iron that pulls it. Both masses accelerate. The mass of the 10-N iron weight is 1 kg—so the total mass being accelerated (cart + iron) is 2 kg. Then,

$$a = \frac{F}{m} = \frac{10\,\text{N}}{2\,\text{kg}} = 5\,\text{m/s}^2.$$

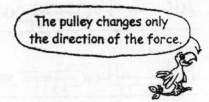
The pulley changes only the direction of the force.

Don't forget: the total mass of a system includes the mass of the hanging iron.

Note this is half the acceleration due to gravity alone, g. So the acceleration of 2 kg produced by the weight of 1 kg is g/2.

a. Find the acceleration of the 1-kg cart when two identical 10-N weights are attached to the string.

$$a = \frac{F}{m} = \frac{\text{applied force}}{\text{total mass}} = \underline{\hspace{1cm}} = \underline{\hspace{1cm}}\ \text{m/s}^2$$

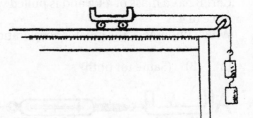

Here we simplify and say g = 10 m/s².

CONCEPTUAL PHYSICS

Drop and Pull—continued

b. Find the acceleration of the 1-kg cart when three identical 10-N weights are attached to the string.

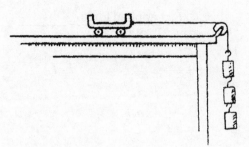

$$a = \frac{F}{m} = \frac{\text{applied force}}{\text{total mass}} = \underline{\hspace{1cm}} = \underline{\hspace{1cm}} \text{ m/s}^2$$

c. Find the acceleration of the 1-kg cart when four identical 10-N weights (not shown) are attached to the string.

$$a = \frac{F}{m} = \frac{\text{applied force}}{\text{total mass}} = \underline{\hspace{1cm}} = \underline{\hspace{1cm}} \text{ m/s}^2$$

d. This time 1 kg of iron is added to the cart, and only one iron piece dangles from the pulley. Find the acceleration of the cart.

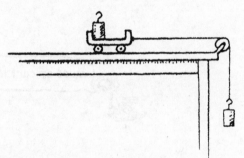

$$a = \frac{F}{m} = \frac{\text{applied force}}{\text{total mass}} = \underline{\hspace{1cm}} = \underline{\hspace{1cm}} \text{ m/s}^2$$

 The force due to gravity on a mass *m* is *mg*.
So gravitational force on 1 kg is (1 kg)(10 m/s²) = 10 N.

e. Find the acceleration of the cart when it carries two pieces of iron and only one iron piece dangles from the pulley.

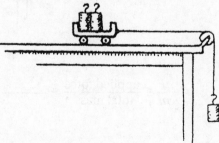

$$a = \frac{F}{m} = \frac{\text{applied force}}{\text{total mass}} = \underline{\hspace{1cm}} = \underline{\hspace{1cm}} \text{ m/s}^2$$

CONCEPTUAL PHYSICS

f. Find the acceleration of the cart when it carries 3 pieces of iron and only one iron piece dangles from the pulley.

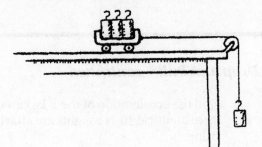

$$a = \frac{F}{m} = \frac{\text{applied force}}{\text{total mass}} = \underline{\hspace{1.5cm}} = \underline{\hspace{1.5cm}} \ \text{m/s}^2$$

g. Find the acceleration of the cart when it carries 3 pieces of iron and 4 pieces of iron dangle from the pulley.

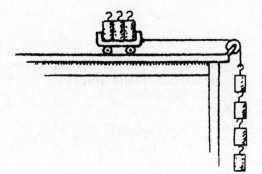

$$a = \frac{F}{m} = \frac{\text{applied force}}{\text{total mass}} = \underline{\hspace{1.5cm}} = \underline{\hspace{1.5cm}} \ \text{m/s}^2$$

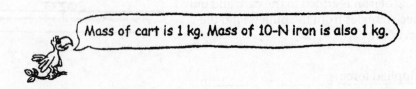

Mass of cart is 1 kg. Mass of 10-N iron is also 1 kg.

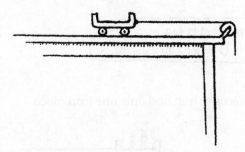

h. Draw your own combination of masses and find the acceleration.

$$a = \frac{F}{m} = \frac{\text{applied force}}{\text{total mass}} = \underline{\hspace{1.5cm}} = \underline{\hspace{1.5cm}} \ \text{m/s}^2$$

CONCEPTUAL PHYSICS

Concept-Development Practice Page | 6-4

Force Vector Components

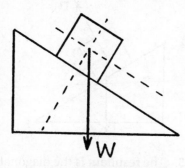

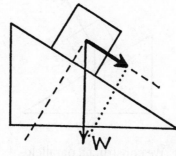

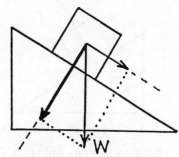

1. The weight of the block is represented by vector **W**. We show axes parallel and perpendicular to the surface of the inclined plane.

2. **W** has a component parallel to the surface (bold vector). Acceleration down the incline is due to this component.

3. **W** also has a component perpendicular to the surface (bold vector). This component gives the force pressing the block against the surface, and is equal and opposite to the normal force (not shown).

4. Here is the same block on a steeper incline. Draw in the components.

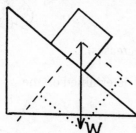

a. For a steeper incline, the component parallel to the incline is (greater) (the same) (less).

b. For a steeper incline, the component perpendicular to the incline (increases) (stays the same) (decreases).

5. Draw components of each weight vector parallel and perpendicular to the surface for the blocks below.

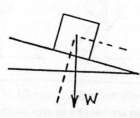 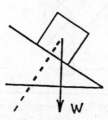 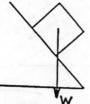 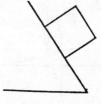

6. A block slides down a friction-free ramp as shown. Construct components of the weight vector: one parallel to the surface at A, B, and C, and the other perpendicular to the surface at these locations.

   a. At which location is the component parallel to the ramp surface greatest? _____

   b. At which location is the acceleration of the block along the ramp greatest? _____

   c. At which location is the acceleration of the block along the ramp least? _____

   d. *True or false:* The speed of the block on this ramp is greatest where acceleration is least. _____

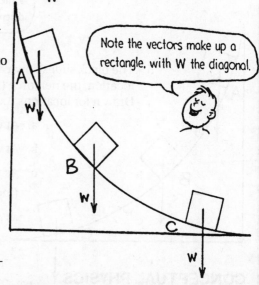

Note the vectors make up a rectangle. with W the diagonal.

CONCEPTUAL PHYSICS

Vector Resultants

On the previous page we considered only the weight vector **W** for a block on a friction-free incline. Here we also consider the normal force **n**.

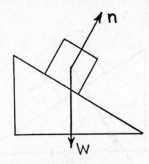 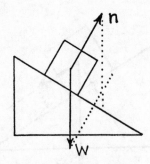 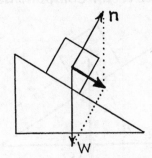

1. With no friction, only two forces act: **W** and **n**. We put the tail of **n** at the block's center to coincide with the tail of **W**—so we can better find the resultant via the parallelogram rule.

2. We construct a parallelogram (dotted lines) whose sides are **W** and **n** to find the resultant **W** + **n**.

3. The resultant is the diagonal as shown (bold vector). This is the net force on the block.

> Net force and acceleration are always in the same direction. Any object accelerating down any incline has a net force parallel to that incline.

4. Note the net forces (bold vectors) for the blocks below.

   a. For a steeper incline, **n** (increases) (stays the same) (decreases).

   b. For a steeper incline, the net force (increases) (stays the same) (decreases).

   c. How does the net force compare to the parallel component of **W** as determined on the previous page? _____

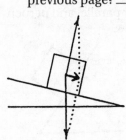 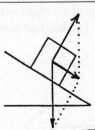 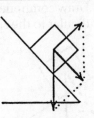 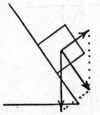 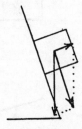

> Without a friction force, the resultant is simply the parallel component of **W** as determined on the previous page. Here we see another way to view the same thing.

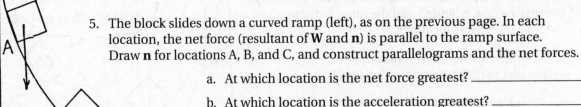

5. The block slides down a curved ramp (left), as on the previous page. In each location, the net force (resultant of **W** and **n**) is parallel to the ramp surface. Draw **n** for locations A, B, and C, and construct parallelograms and the net forces.

   a. At which location is the net force greatest? _____

   b. At which location is the acceleration greatest? _____

   c. As the speed of the block increases, acceleration (increases) (is constant) (decreases).

6. On inclined *flat* planes, acceleration down the incline (is constant) (varies). On curved inclines, acceleration (is constant) (varies).

CONCEPTUAL PHYSICS

Concept-Development Practice Page | 6-5

Equilibrium on an Inclined Plane

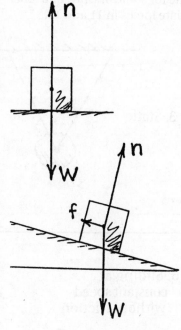

1. The block is at rest on a horizontal surface. The normal support force **n** is equal and opposite to weight **W**.

   a. There is (friction) (no friction) because the block has no tendency to slide.

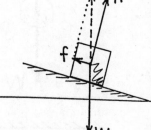

2. At rest on the incline, friction acts. Note (right) the resultant **f + n** (dashed vector) is equal and opposite to **W**.

   a. Here we see that the size of **n** is (less than) (equal to) (greater than) the size of **W.**

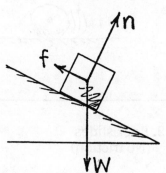

3. Draw the resultant **f + n** for the block at rest on the steeper incline.

   a. The resultant magnitude of **f + n** is (less than) (equal to) (greater than) the magnitude of **W**.

   b. As the angle of the incline increases, the magnitude of vector **n** (decreases) (stays the same) (increases).

4. The block remains at rest on the still steeper incline. Draw vectors for equilibrium.

   a. How does the resultant **f + n** compare to **W**?

   _____

Can you also see that n + W = -f? And f + W = -n? Vectors make sense!

   b. Suppose the angle is increased and the block slides down the incline at constant velocity. Then the net force on the block is (zero) (greater than zero). If the angle is increased even further, then acceleration (occurs) (doesn't occur).

5. Further steepness of the incline means (less) (more) acceleration down the plane. When the incline is vertical, acceleration is (less than g) (g) (more than g).

CONCEPTUAL PHYSICS

Force-Vector Diagrams

In each case, a rock is acted on by one or more forces. Draw an accurate vector diagram showing all forces acting on the rock, and no other forces. Use a ruler, and do it in pencil so you can correct mistakes. The first two are done as examples. Show by the parallelogram rule in 2 that the vector sum of **A** + **B** is equal and opposite to **W** (that is, **A** + **B** = -**W**). Do the same for 3 and 4. Draw and label vectors for the weight and normal forces in 5 to 10, and for the appropriate forces in 11 and 12.

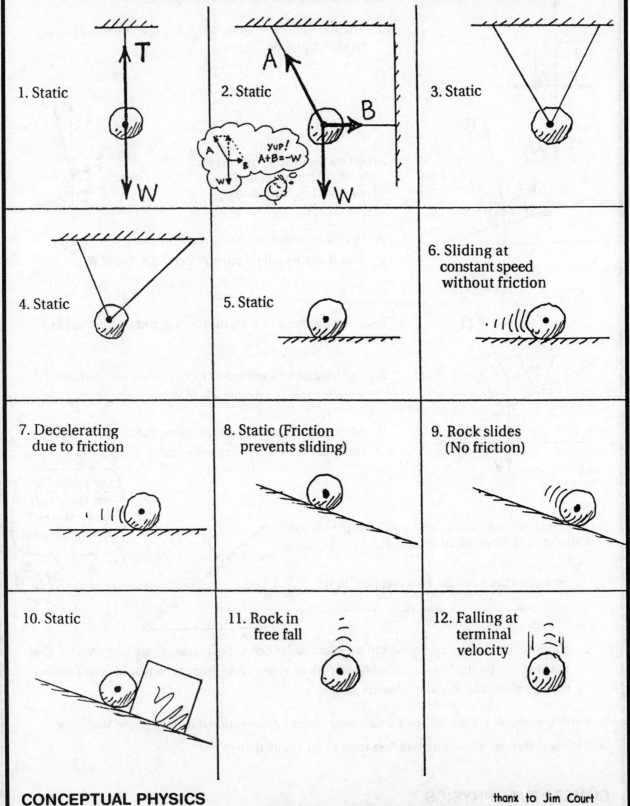

1. Static

2. Static

   yup! A+B=-W

3. Static

4. Static

5. Static

6. Sliding at constant speed without friction

7. Decelerating due to friction

8. Static (Friction prevents sliding)

9. Rock slides (No friction)

10. Static

11. Rock in free fall

12. Falling at terminal velocity

CONCEPTUAL PHYSICS

thanx to Jim Court

Concept-Development Practice Page | 6-6

Sailboats

(Do not attempt this until you have studied Appendix D!)

1. The sketch shows a top view of a small railroad car pulled by a rope. The force **F** that the rope exerts on the car has one component along the track, and another component perpendicular to the track.

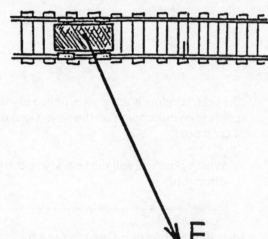

   a. Draw these components on the sketch. Which component is larger?

   _____

   b. Which component produces acceleration?

   _____

   c. What would be the effect of pulling on the rope if it were perpendicular to the track?

   _____

2. The sketches below represent simplified top views of sailboats in cross-wind direction. The impact of the wind produces a FORCE vector on each as shown. (We do NOT consider *velocity* vectors here!)

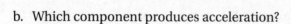

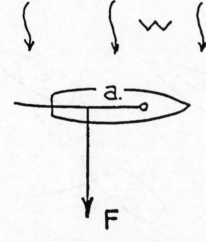

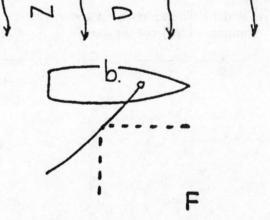

   a. Why is the position of the sail above useless for propelling the boat along its forward direction? (Relate this to Question 1c above. Where the train is constrained by tracks to move in one direction, the boat is similarly constrained to move along one direction by its deep vertical fin — the *keel*.)

   _____

   _____

   b. Sketch the component of force parallel to the direction of the boat's motion (along its keel), and the component perpendicular to its motion. Will the boat move in a forward direction? (Relate this to Question 1b above.)

   _____

   _____

CONCEPTUAL PHYSICS

3. The boat to the right is oriented at an angle into the wind. Draw the force vector and its forward and perpendicular components.

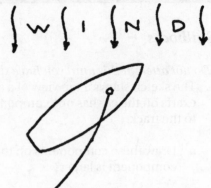

a. Will the boat move in a forward direction and tack into the wind? Why or why not?

_____

_____

4. The sketch below is a top view of five identical sailboats. Where they exist, draw force vectors to represent wind impact on the sails. Then draw components parallel and perpendicular to the keels of each boat.

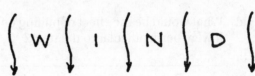

a. Which boat will sail the fastest in a forward direction?

_____

b. Which will respond least to the wind?

_____

c. Which will move in a backward direction?

_____

d. Which will experience less and less wind impact with increasing speed?

_____

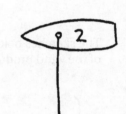

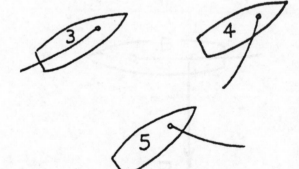

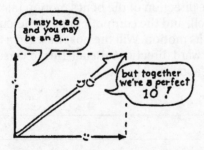

I may be a 6 and you may be an 8... but together we're a perfect 10 !

Force and Velocity Vectors

1. Draw sample vectors to represent the force of gravity on the ball in the positions shown above (after it leaves the thrower's hand). Neglect air drag.

2. Draw sample bold vectors to represent the velocity of the ball in the positions shown above. With lighter vectors, show the horizontal and vertical components of velocity for each position.

3. a. Which velocity component in the previous question remains constant ? Why?

   _____

   b. Which velocity component changes along the path? Why?

   _____

4. It is important to distinguish between force and velocity vectors. Force vectors combine with other force vectors, and velocity vectors combine with other velocity vectors. Do velocity vectors combine with force vectors? _____

5. All forces on the bowling ball, weight down and support of alley up, are shown by vectors at its center before it strikes the pin (a). Draw vectors of all the forces that act on the ball (b) when it strikes the pin, and (c) after it strikes the pin.

a    b    c

CONCEPTUAL PHYSICS

thanx to Howard Brand

Concept-Development Practice Page 7-2

Newton's Third Law

1. In the example below, the action-reaction pair is shown by the arrows (vectors), and the action-reaction described in words. In (a) through (g) draw the other arrow (vector) and state the reaction to the given action. Then make up your own example in (h).

Example:

Fist hits wall

Wall hits fist

Head bumps ball

a. _____

Windshield hits bug

b. _____

Bat hits ball

c. _____

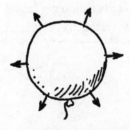

Hand touches nose

d. _____

Hand pulls on flower

e. _____

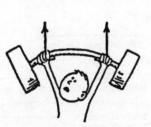

Athlete pushes bar upward

f. _____
   _____

Compressed air pushes balloon surface outward

g. _____
   _____

h. _____
   _____
   _____

2. Draw arrows to show the chain of at least six pairs of action-reaction forces below.

YOU CAN'T TOUCH WITHOUT BEING TOUCHED— NEWTON'S THIRD LAW

CONCEPTUAL PHYSICS

3. Nellie Newton holds an apple weighing 1 newton at rest on the palm of her hand. The force vectors shown are the forces that act on the apple.

a. To say the weight of the apple is 1 N is to say that a downward gravitational force of 1 N is exerted on the apple by (Earth) (her hand).

b. Nellie's hand supports the apple with normal force **n**, which acts in a direction opposite to **W**. We can say **n** (equals **W**) (has the same magnitude as **W**).

c. Since the apple is at rest, the net force on the apple is (zero) (nonzero).

d. Since **n** is equal and opposite to **W**, we (can) (cannot) say that **n** and **W** comprise an action-reaction pair. The reason is because action and reaction always (act on the same object) (act on different objects), and here we see **n** and **W** (both acting on the apple) (acting on different objects).

e. In accord with the rule, "If ACTION is A acting on B, then REACTION is B acting on A," if we say *action* is Earth pulling down on the apple, *reaction* is (the apple pulling up on Earth) (**n**, Nellie's hand pushing up on the apple).

f. To repeat for emphasis, we see that **n** and **W** are equal and opposite to each other (and comprise an action-reaction pair) (but do *not* comprise an action-reaction pair).

To identify a pair of action-reaction forces in any situation, first identify the pair of interacting objects involved. Something is interacting with something else. In this case the whole Earth is interacting (gravitationally) with the apple. So Earth pulls downward on the apple (call it action), while the apple pulls upward on Earth (reaction).

Simply put: Earth pulls on apple (action); apple pulls on Earth (reaction).

Better put: Apple and Earth *pull on each other* with equal and opposite forces that comprise a *single* interaction.

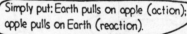

g. Another pair of forces is **n** [shown] and the downward force of the apple against Nellie's hand [not shown]. This force pair (is) (isn't) an action-reaction pair.

h. Suppose Nellie now pushes upward on the apple with a force of 2 N. The apple (is still in equilibrium) (accelerates upward), and compared to **W**, the magnitude of **n** is (the same) (twice) (not the same, and not twice).

i. Once the apple leaves Nellie's hand, **n** is (zero) (still twice the magnitude of **W**), and the net force on the apple is (zero) (only **W**) (still **W** – **n**, which is a negative force).

Momentum

1. A moving car has momentum. If it moves twice as fast, its momentum

   is _____ as much.

2. Two cars, one twice as heavy as the other, move down a hill at the same speed. Compared to the

   lighter car, the momentum of the heavier car is _____ as much.

3. The recoil momentum of a cannon that kicks is

   (more than)   (less than)   (the same as)

   the momentum of the cannonball it fires.

4. If a man firmly holds a cannon when fired, then the momentum of the cannonball is equal to
   the recoil momentum of the

   (cannon alone)   (cannon–man system)   (man alone).

5. Suppose you are traveling in a bus at highway speed on a nice summer day and the momentum of
   an unlucky bug is suddenly changed as it splatters onto the front window.

   a. Compared to the force that acts on the bug,
      how much force acts on the bus?

      (more)   (the same)   (less).

   b. The time of impact is the same for both the bug
      and the bus. Compared to the impulse on the
      bug, this means the impulse on the bus is

      (more)   (the same)   (less).

   c. Although the momentum of the bus is very
      large compared to the momentum of the
      bug, the *change* in momentum of the bus,
      compared to the *change* of momentum of the
      bug is

      (more)   (the same)   (less).

   d. Which undergoes the greater acceleration?

      (Bus)   (Both the same)   (Bug)

   e. Which, therefore, suffers the greater damage?

      (Bus)   (Both the same)   (The bug of course!)

CONCEPTUAL PHYSICS

6. Granny whizzes around the rink and is suddenly confronted with Ambrose at rest directly in her path. Rather than knock him over, she picks him up and continues in motion without "braking."

Consider both Granny and Ambrose as two parts of one system. Since no outside forces act on the system, the momentum of the system before collision equals the momentum of the system after collision.

a. Complete the before-collision data in the table below.

BEFORE COLLISION	
Granny's mass	80 kg
Granny's speed	3 m/s
Granny's momentum	_____
Ambrose's mass	40 kg
Ambrose's speed	0 m/s
Ambrose's momentum	_____
Total momentum	_____

b. After collision, does Granny's speed increase or decrease?

_____

c. After collision, does Ambrose's speed increase or decrease?

_____

d. After collision, what is the total mass of Granny + Ambrose?

_____

e. After collision, what is the total momentum of Granny + Ambrose?

_____

f. Use the conservation of momentum law to find the speed of Granny and Ambrose together after collision. (Show your work in the space below.)

New speed = _____

CONCEPTUAL PHYSICS

Systems

1. When the compressed spring is released, Blocks A and B will slide apart. There are 3 systems to consider, indicated by the closed dashed lines below—A, B, and A + B. Ignore the vertical forces of gravity and the support force of the table.

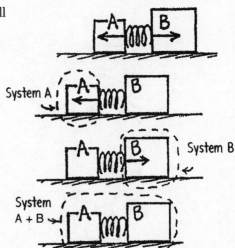

   a. Does an external force act on System A? (Y) (N)

   Will the momentum of System A change? (Y) (N)

   b. Does an external force act on System B? (Y) (N)

   Will the momentum of System B change? (Y) (N)

   c. Does an external force act on System A + B? (Y) (N)

   Will the momentum of System A + B change? (Y) (N)

2. Billiard ball A collides with billiard ball B at rest. Isolate each system with a closed dashed line. Draw only the external force vectors that act on each system.

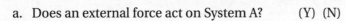

   System A   System B   System A + B

Note that external forces on System A and System B are internal to System A+B, so they cancel!

   a. Upon collision, the momentum of System A   (increases) (decreases) (remains unchanged).

   b. Upon collision, the momentum of System B   (increases) (decreases) (remains unchanged).

   c. Upon collision, the momentum of System A + B (increases) (decreases) (remains unchanged).

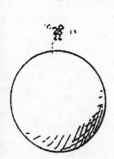

3. a. A girl jumps upward. In the left sketch, draw a closed dashed line to indicate the system of the girl. Is there an external force acting on her? (Y) (N)

   Does her momentum change? (Y) (N)

   Is the girl's momentum conserved? (Y) (N)

   b. In the right sketch, draw a closed dashed line to indicate the system (girl + Earth). Is there an external force acting on the system due to the interaction between the girl and Earth? (Y) (N)

4. A block strikes a blob of jelly. Isolate 3 systems with a closed dashed line and show the external force on each. In which system is momentum conserved?

5. A truck crashes into a wall. Isolate 3 systems with a closed dashed line and show the external force on each. In which system is momentum conserved?

CONCEPTUAL PHYSICS

thanx to Cedric Linder

Concept-Development
Practice Page

9-1

Work and Energy

1. How much work (energy) is needed to lift an object that weighs 200 N to a height of 4 m?

   _____

2. How much power is needed to lift the 200-N object to a height of 4 m in 4 s?

   _____

3. What is the power output of an engine that does 60,000 J of work in 10 s?

   _____

4. The block of ice weighs 500 newtons.

   a. What is the mechanical advantage of the incline?

   _____

   b. How much force is needed to push it up the incline (neglect friction)?

   _____

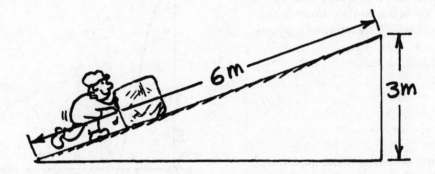

5. All the ramps are 5 m high. We know that the KE of the block at the bottom of the ramp will be equal to the loss of PE (conservation of energy). Find the speed of the block at ground level in each case. [*Hint*: Do you recall from earlier chapters how long it takes something to fall a vertical distance of 5 m from a position of rest (assume $g = 10$ m/s^2)? And how much speed a falling object acquires in this time? This gives you the answer to Case 1. Discuss with your classmates how energy conservation gives you the answers to Cases 2 and 3.]

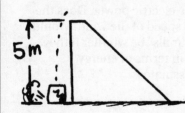  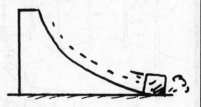

Case 1: Speed = _____ m/s   Case 2: Speed = _____ m/s   Case 3: Speed = _____ m/s

CONCEPTUAL PHYSICS

6. Which block gets to the bottom of the incline first? Assume no friction. (Be careful!) Explain your answer.

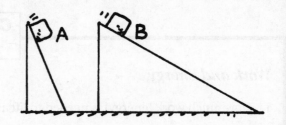

_____

_____

_____

7. The KE and PE of a block freely sliding down a ramp are shown in only one place in the sketch. Fill in the missing values.

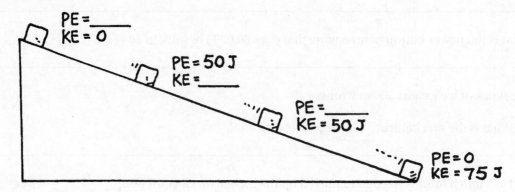

PE = _____
KE = 0

PE = 50 J
KE = _____

PE = _____
KE = 50 J

PE = 0
KE = 75 J

8. A big metal bead slides due to gravity along an upright friction-free wire. It starts from rest at the top of the wire as shown in the sketch. How fast is it traveling as it passes

Point B? _____

Point D? _____

Point E? _____

At what point does it have the maximum speed? _____

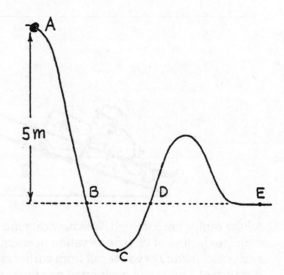

9. Rows of wind-powered generators are used in various windy locations to generate electric power. Does the power generated affect the speed of the wind? Would locations behind the "windmills" be windier if they weren't there? Discuss this in terms of energy conservation with your classmates.

_____

_____

_____

_____

_____

CONCEPTUAL PHYSICS

Concept-Development Practice Page · 9-2

Conservation of Energy

1. Fill in the blanks for the six systems shown.

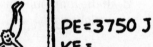

PE = 15000 J
KE = 0

PE = 30 J

PE = _____

PE = _____

PE = _____

KE = _____

PE = 11250 J
KE = _____

PE = 7500 J
KE = _____

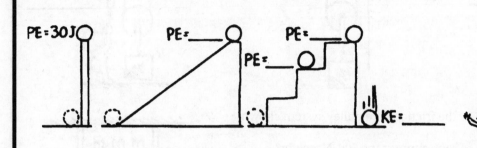

υ = 30 km/h
KE = 10⁶ J

υ = 60 km/h
KE = _____

υ = 90 km/h
KE = _____

PE = 3750 J
KE = _____

PE = 10⁴ J

WORK DONE = _____

PE = _____
KE = 0

PE = 25 J
KE = _____

PE = 0 J
KE = _____

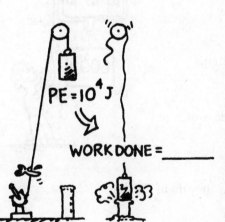

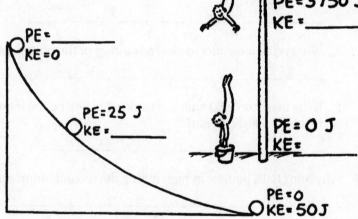

PE = 0
KE = 50 J

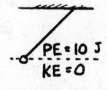

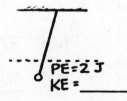

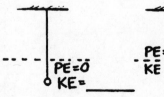

PE = 10 J
KE = 0

PE = 2 J
KE = _____

PE = 0
KE = _____

PE = _____
KE = _____

CONCEPTUAL PHYSICS

2. The woman supports a 100-N load with the friction-free pulley systems shown below. Fill in the spring-scale readings that show how much force she must exert.

  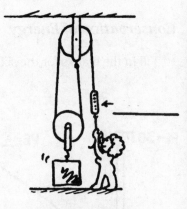

3. A 600-N block is lifted by the friction-free pulley system shown.

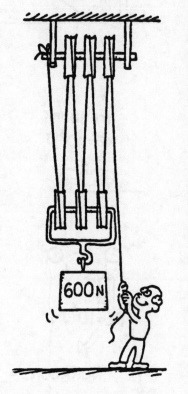

   a. How many strands of rope support the 600-N weight?

   _____

   b. What is the tension in each strand?

   _____

   c. What is the tension in the end held by the man?

   _____

   d. If the man pulls his end down 60 cm, how many cm will the weight rise?

   _____

   e. What is the ideal mechanical advantage of the pulley system?

   _____

   f. If the man exerts 60 joules of work, what will be the increase of PE of the 600-N weight?

   _____

4. Why don't balls bounce as high during the second bounce as they do in the first?

   _____

   _____

   _____

CONCEPTUAL PHYSICS

Concept-Development Practice Page 9-3

Momentum and Energy

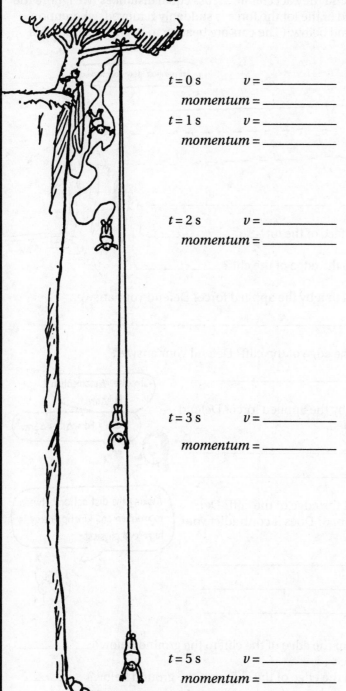

t = 0 s   v = _____

momentum = _____

t = 1 s   v = _____

momentum = _____

t = 2 s   v = _____

momentum = _____

t = 3 s   v = _____

momentum = _____

t = 5 s   v = _____

momentum = _____

Bronco Brown wants to put $Ft = \Delta mv$ to the test and try bungee jumping. Bronco leaps from a high cliff and experiences free fall for 3 seconds. Then the bungee cord begins to stretch, reducing his speed to zero in 2 seconds. Fortunately, the cord stretches to its maximum length just short of the ground below.

Fill in the blanks. Bronco's mass is 100 kg. Acceleration of free fall is 10 m/s².

Express values in SI units (*distance* in m, *velocity* in m/s, *momentum* in kg·m/s, *impulse* in N·s, and *deceleration* in m/s²).

The 3-s free-fall distance of Bronco just before the bungee cord begins to stretch

= _____.

Δmv during the 3-s interval of free fall

= _____.

Δmv during the 2-s interval of slowing down

= _____.

Impulse during the 2-s interval of slowing down

= _____.

Average force exerted by the cord during the 2-s interval of slowing down

= _____.

How about *work* and *energy?* How much KE does Bronco have 3 s after his jump?

_____

How much does gravitational PE decrease during this 3 s?

_____

What two kinds of PE are changing during the slowing-down interval?

_____

CONCEPTUAL PHYSICS

Energy and Momentum

A compact car and a full-size sedan are initially at rest on a horizontal parking lot at the edge of a steep cliff. For simplicity, we assume that the sedan has twice as much mass as the compact car. Equal constant forces are applied to each car and they accelerate across equal distances (we ignore the effects of friction). When they reach the far end of the lot the force is suddenly removed, whereupon they sail through the air and crash to the ground below. (The cars are beat up to begin with, and this is a scientific experiment!)

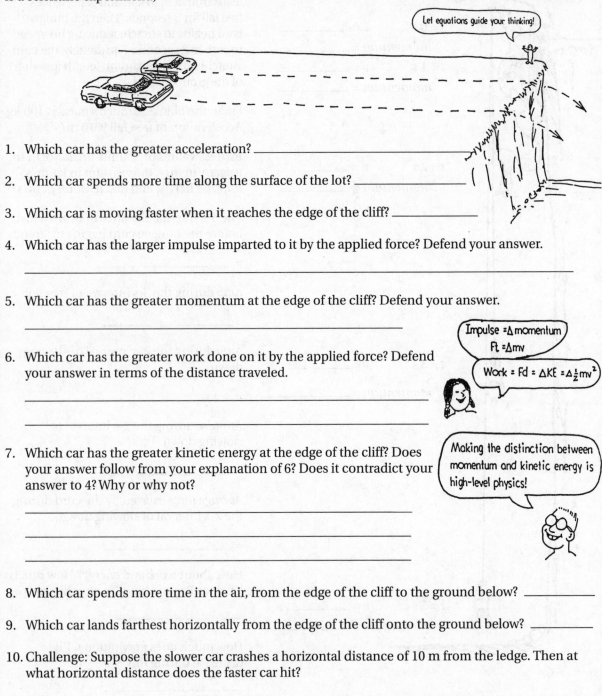

Let equations guide your thinking!

1. Which car has the greater acceleration? _____

2. Which car spends more time along the surface of the lot? _____

3. Which car is moving faster when it reaches the edge of the cliff? _____

4. Which car has the larger impulse imparted to it by the applied force? Defend your answer.

   _____

5. Which car has the greater momentum at the edge of the cliff? Defend your answer.

   _____

6. Which car has the greater work done on it by the applied force? Defend your answer in terms of the distance traveled.

   _____

   _____

   Impulse $= \Delta$ momentum
   $Ft = \Delta mv$

   Work $= Fd = \Delta KE = \Delta \frac{1}{2}mv^2$

7. Which car has the greater kinetic energy at the edge of the cliff? Does your answer follow from your explanation of 6? Does it contradict your answer to 4? Why or why not?

   _____

   _____

   _____

   Making the distinction between momentum and kinetic energy is high-level physics!

8. Which car spends more time in the air, from the edge of the cliff to the ground below? _____

9. Which car lands farthest horizontally from the edge of the cliff onto the ground below? _____

10. Challenge: Suppose the slower car crashes a horizontal distance of 10 m from the ledge. Then at what horizontal distance does the faster car hit?

    _____

    _____

CONCEPTUAL PHYSICS

Concept-Development Practice Page **10-1**

Acceleration and Circular Motion

Newton's second law, $a = F/m$, tells us that net force and its corresponding acceleration are always in the same direction. (Both force and acceleration are vector quantities.) But force and acceleration are not always in the direction of velocity (another vector).

1. You're in a car at a traffic light. The light turns green and the driver "steps on the gas."

   a. Your body lurches (forward) (not at all) (backward).

   b. The car accelerates (forward) (not at all) (backward).

   c. The force on the car acts (forward) (not at all) (backward).

   The sketch shows the top view of the car. Note the directions of the velocity and acceleration vectors.

2. You're driving along and approach a stop sign. The driver steps on the brakes.

   a. Your body lurches (forward) (not at all) (backward).

   b. The car accelerates (forward) (not at all) (backward).

   c. The force on the car acts (forward) (not at all) (backward).

   The sketch shows the top view of the car. Draw vectors for velocity and acceleration.

3. You continue driving, and round a sharp curve to the left at constant speed.

   a. Your body leans (inward) (not at all) (outward).

   b. The direction of the car's acceleration is (inward) (not at all) (outward).

   c. The force on the car acts (inward) (not at all) (outward).

   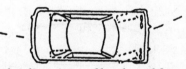

   Draw vectors for velocity and acceleration of the car.

4. In general, the directions of lurch and acceleration, and therefore the directions of lurch and force, are (the same) (not related) (opposite).

5. The whirling stone's direction of motion keeps changing.

   a. If it moves faster, its direction changes (faster) (slower).

   b. This indicates that as speed increases, acceleration (increases) (decreases) (stays the same).

6. Consider whirling the stone on a shorter string—that is, of smaller radius.

   a. For a given speed, the rate that the stone changes direction is (less) (more) (the same).

   b. This indicates that as the radius decreases, acceleration (increases) (decreases) (stays the same).

CONCEPTUAL PHYSICS

Centripetal Force

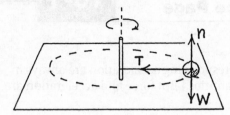

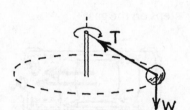

1. A rock tied to a post moves in a circle at constant speed on a frictionless horizontal surface. All the forces acting on the rock are shown: Tension **T**, support force **n** by the table, and the force due to gravity **W**.

   a. The vector responsible for circular motion is _____.

   b. The net force on the rock is _____.

2. In this case the rock is tied to a string and swings in a circular path as shown. It is not resting on a surface so there is no friction. Use the parallelogram rule and find the resultant of vectors **T** and **W**.

   a. What is the direction of the resultant of **T** and **W**? _____

   b. Does this resultant lie in the plane of the circular path? _____

   c. Is this resultant also the horizontal component of **T**? _____

   d. Is the resultant **T** + **W** (or the horizontal component of **T**) a centripetal force? _____

3. In the case shown at the right, the rock rides on a horizontal disk that rotates at constant speed about its vertical axis (dotted line). Friction prevents the rock from sliding.

   a. Draw and label vectors for all forces that act on the rock.

   b. Which force is centripetal? _____

   c. Which force provides the net force? _____

   d. Why do we *not* say the net force is zero? _____

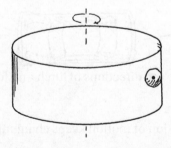

4. Now the rock is held in place by friction against the inside wall of the rotating drum. Draw and label vectors for all forces that act on the rock.

   a. Which force is centripetal? _____

   b. Which force provides the net force? _____

5. More challenging: This time the rock rests against the frictionless inside wall of a cone. It moves with the cone, which rotates about its vertical axis (dotted line). The rock does not slide up or down in the cone as it rotates. Draw and label vectors for all forces that act on the rock.

   Should the resultant force lie in the plane of the circular path? _____

   Why? _____

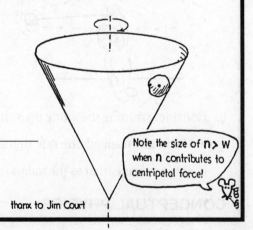

Note the size of **n** > **W** when **n** contributes to centripetal force!

The Flying Pig

The toy pig flies in a circle at constant speed. This arrangement is called a conical pendulum because the supporting string sweeps out a cone. Neglecting the action of its flapping wings, only two forces act on the pig—gravitational $m\mathbf{g}$, and string tension $\mathbf{T}$.

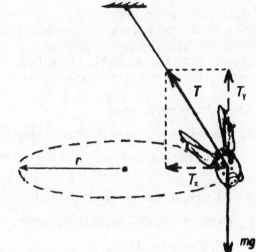

Vector Component Analysis:
Note that vector $\mathbf{T}$ can be resolved into two components—horizontal $\mathbf{T}_x$, and vertical $\mathbf{T}_y$. These vector components are dashed to distinguish them from the tension vector $\mathbf{T}$.

Circle the correct answers.

1. If $\mathbf{T}$ were somehow replaced with $\mathbf{T}_x$ and $\mathbf{T}_y$ the pig (would) (would not) behave identically to being supported by $\mathbf{T}$.

2. Since the pig doesn't accelerate vertically, compared with the magnitude of $m\mathbf{g}$, component $\mathbf{T}_y$, must be (greater) (less) (equal and opposite).

3. The velocity of the pig at any instant is (along the radius of) (tangent to) its circular path.

4. Since the pig continues in circular motion, component $\mathbf{T}_x$ must be a (centripetal) (centrifugal) (nonexistent) force, which equals (zero) (mv^2/r). Furthermore, $\mathbf{T}_x$ is (along the radius of) (tangent to) the circle swept out.

Vector Resultant Analysis:
5. Rather than resolving $\mathbf{T}$ into horizontal and vertical components, use your pencil to sketch the resultant of $m\mathbf{g}$ and $\mathbf{T}$ using the *parallelogram rule.*

6. The resultant lies in a (horizontal) (vertical) direction, and (toward) (away from) the center of the circular path. The resultant of $m\mathbf{g}$ and $\mathbf{T}$ is a (centripetal) (centrifugal) force.

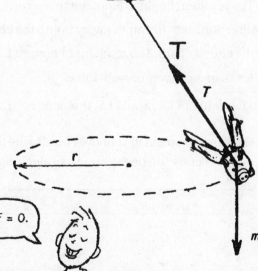

For straight-line motion with no acceleration, $\Sigma F = 0$. But for uniform circular motion, $\Sigma F = mv^2/r$.

thanx to Pablo Robinson and Miss Piggy

CONCEPTUAL PHYSICS

Banked Airplanes

An airplane banks as it turns along a horizontal circular path in the air. Except for the thrust of its engines and air resistance, the two significant forces on the plane are gravitational *mg* (vertical), and lift **L** (perpendicular to the wings).

Vector Component Analysis:
With a ruler and a pencil, resolve vector **L** into two perpendicular components, horizontal $\mathbf{L}_x$, and vertical $\mathbf{L}_y$. Make these vectors dashed to distinguish them from **L**.

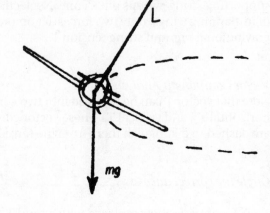

Circle the correct answers.

1. The velocity of the airplane at any instant is

   (along the radius of) (tangent to) its circular path.

2. If **L** were somehow replaced with $\mathbf{L}_x$ and $\mathbf{L}_y$, the

   airplane (would) (would not) behave the same as

   being supported by **L**.

3. Since the airplane doesn't accelerate vertically, component $\mathbf{L}_y$ must be

   (greater than) (less than) (equal and opposite to) *mg*.

4. Since the plane continues in circular motion, component $\mathbf{L}_x$ must equal (zero) (mv^2/r) , and be a

   (centripetal) (centrifugal) (nonexistent) force. Furthermore, $\mathbf{L}_x$ is

   (along the radius of) (tangent to) the circular path.

Vector Resultant Analysis:

5. Rather than resolving **L** into horizontal and vertical components, use your pencil to sketch the resultant of *mg* and **L** using the *parallelogram rule*.

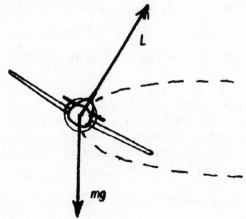

6. The resultant lies in a (horizontal) (vertical)

   direction, and (toward) (away from) the center of

   the circular path. The resultant of *mg* and **L** is a

   (centripetal) (centrifugal) force.

7. The resultant of *mg* and **L** is the same as $(\mathbf{L}_x)$ $(\mathbf{L}_y)$.

8. Challenge: Explain in your own words why the resultant of two vectors can be the same as a single component of one of them.

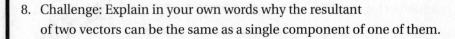

_____

CONCEPTUAL PHYSICS

Banked Track

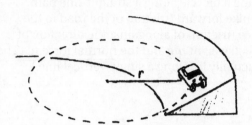

A car rounds a banked curve with just the right speed so that it has no tendency to slide down or up the banked road surface. Shown below are two main forces that act on the car perpendicular to its motion—gravitational mg and the normal force **n** (the support force of the surface).

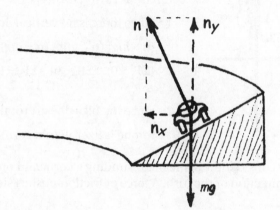

Vector Component Analysis:
Note that vector **n** is resolved into two perpendicular components, horizontal $\mathbf{n}_x$ and vertical $\mathbf{n}_y$. As usual, these vectors are dashed to distinguish them from **n**.

Circle the correct answers.

1. If **n** were somehow replaced with

   $\mathbf{n}_x$ and $\mathbf{n}_y$, the car (would) (would not)

   behave identically to being supported by **n**.

2. Since the car doesn't accelerate vertically, component $\mathbf{n}_y$ must be

   (greater than) (equal and opposite to) (less than) mg.

3. The velocity of the car at any instant is (along the radius of) (tangent to) its circular path.

4. Since the car continues in uniform circular motion, component $\mathbf{n}_x$ must equal (zero) (mv^2/r)

   and be a (centripetal) (centrifugal) (nonexistent) force. Furthermore, $\mathbf{n}_x$ is

   (along the radius of) (tangent to) the circular path.

Vector Resultant Analysis:
5. Rather than resolving **n** into horizontal and vertical components, use your pencil to sketch the resultant of mg and **n** using the *parallelogram rule.*

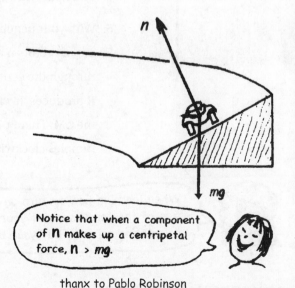

6. The resultant lies in a (horizontal) (vertical)

   direction, and (toward) (away from) the

   center of the circular path. The resultant of

   mg and **n** is a (centripetal) (centrifugal) force.

7. The resultant of mg and **n** is the same

   as ($\mathbf{n}_x$) ($\mathbf{n}_y$), and provides the

   (centripetal) (centrifugal) force.

> Notice that when a component of **n** makes up a centripetal force, **n** > mg.

thanx to Pablo Robinson

CONCEPTUAL PHYSICS

Leaning

When turning a corner on a bicycle, everyone knows that you've got to lean "into the curve." What is the physics of this leaning? It involves torque, friction, and centripetal force (mv^2/r).

First, consider the simple case of riding a bicycle along a straight-line path. Except for the force that propels the bike forward (friction of the road in the direction of motion) and air resistance (friction of air against the direction of motion), only two significant forces act: weight mg and the normal force **n**. (The vectors are drawn side-by-side, but actually lie along a single vertical line.)

Circle the correct answers.

1. Since there is no vertical acceleration, we can say that the magnitude of
   ($\mathbf{n} > mg$) ($\mathbf{n} < mg$) ($\mathbf{n} = mg$), which means that in the vertical direction,
   ($\Sigma F_y > 0$) ($\Sigma F_y < 0$) ($\Sigma F_y = 0$).

2. Since the bike doesn't rotate or change in its rotational state, then the total torque is (zero) (not zero).

Now consider the same bike rounding a corner. In order to safely make the turn, the bicyclist leans in the direction of the turn. A force of friction pushes sideways on the tire toward the center of the curve.

3. The friction force, **f**, provides the centripetal force that produces a curved path. Then ($\mathbf{f} = mv^2/r$) ($\mathbf{f} \neq mv^2/r$).

4. Consider the net torque about the center of mass (CM) of the bike-rider system. Gravity produces no torque about this point, but **n** and **f** do. The torque involving **n** tends to produce (clockwise) (counterclockwise) rotation, and the one involving **f** tends to produce (clockwise) (counterclockwise) rotation.
   These torques cancel each other when the resultant of vectors **n** and **f** pass through the CM.

5. With your pencil, use the parallelogram rule and sketch in the result-ant of vectors **n** and **f**. Label your resultant **R**. Note the **R** passes through the center of mass of the bike-rider system. That means that **R** produces (a clockwise) (a counterclockwise) (no) torque about the CM. Therefore the bike-rider system (topples clockwise) (topples counterclockwise) (doesn't topple).

When learning how to turn on a bike, you lean so that the sum of the torques about your CM is zero. You may not be calculating torques, but your body learns to feel them.

thanx to Pablo Robinson

CONCEPTUAL PHYSICS

Concept-Development Practice Page **11-1**

Torques

1. Felix Flex pulls the bar forward, rotates the cam, and lifts the load. Two torques act on the cam—the counterclockwise torque produced by Felix's pull **P**, and the clockwise torque produced by the tension **T** that supports the load: Note that although **T** stays constant, the torque is not constant because of the variable lever arm (hence the cam's odd shape!).

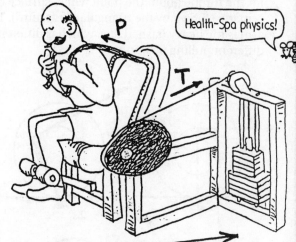

Shown below is the cam in three positions, A, B, and C. The lever arm (heavy dashed line) is shown for position A.

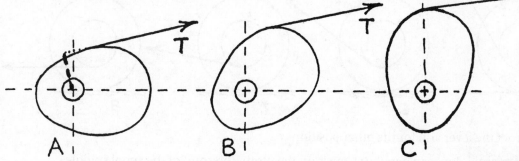

a. Draw the different-length lever arms for positions B and C. (Take care that your lever arm is perpendicular to the line of action of **T**!)

b. In which position does the cam provide the longest lever arm? _____

c. In which position does **T** produce the greatest torque? _____

d. In which position does the cam provide the shortest lever arm? _____

e. In which position does **T** produce the least torque? _____

f. Which position requires the least pull **P** for Felix to rotate? _____

g. Which position requires the most pull **P** for Felix to rotate? _____

Note that (**P** x lever arm between **P** and cam axis) = (**T** x lever arm constructed in a)

Tension **T** = weight of the load, whether the load is held stationary or moved at constant speed.

The torque Felix produces on the cam depends on his pull **P**, which in turn depends on the cam position.

CONCEPTUAL PHYSICS

thanx to Manuel Hewitt

2. Pull the string gently and the spool rolls. The direction of roll depends on the way the torque is applied.

In (1) and (2) below, the force and lever arm are shown for the torque about the point where surface contact is made (shown by the triangular "fulcrum"). The lever arm is the heavy dashed line, which is different for each different pulling position.

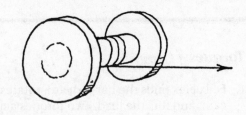

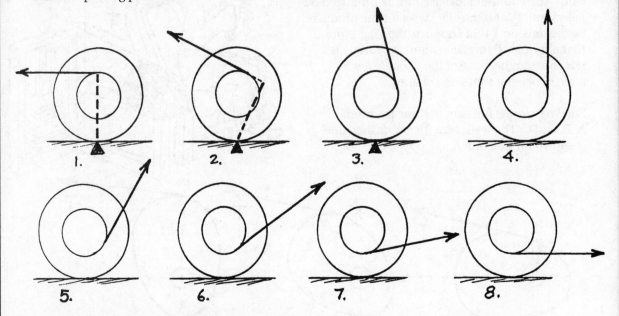

a. Construct the lever arm for the other positions.

b. The lever arm is longer when the string is on the (top) (bottom) of the spool spindle.

c. For a given pull, the torque is greater when the string is on the (top) (bottom).

d. For the same pull, rotational acceleration is greater when the string is on the (top) (bottom) (makes no difference).

e. At which positions does the spool roll to the left? _____

f. At which positions does the spool roll to the right? _____

g. At which position does the spool not roll at all? _____

h. Why does the spool slide rather than roll at this position?

_____

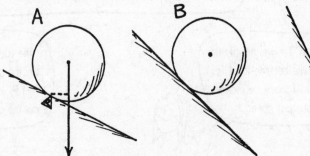

Be sure your right angle is between the force's *line of action* and the lever arm.

3. We all know that a ball rolls down an incline. But relatively few people know that the reason the ball picks up rotational speed is because of a torque. In Sketch A, we see the ingredients of the torque acting on the ball—the force due to gravity and the lever arm to the point where surface contact is made.

a. Construct the lever arms for positions B and C.

b. As the incline becomes steeper, the torque

(increases) (decreases)

(remains the same).

A   B   C

CONCEPTUAL PHYSICS

Concept-Development Practice Page **11-2**

Center of Gravity

1. Which bottle is the most stable? _____

least stable? _____

neutral? _____

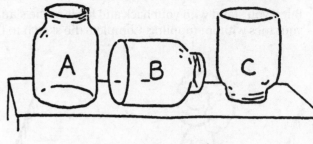

2. Draw vectors for the weight of each truck.

Which truck will tip over? _____

Why? _____

_____

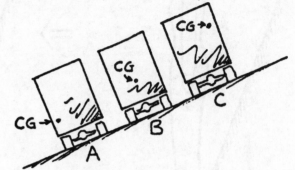

3. Both blocks have equal mass. Which

requires more work to tip over? _____

Why? _____

_____

4. Why or why not will the pipe tip over?

_____

_____

5. The wheels of a bike provide two points of contact
with the ground. A kick stand provides a third. Sketch
in the triangular area bounded by the three points
of ground contact. Where is the CG of the bike with
respect to this area?

_____

_____

CONCEPTUAL PHYSICS

6. Ordinarily when you stand with your back and heels to a wall, you cannot bend over and touch your toes without toppling forward. Why?

_____

But if you stand with your back and heels to the slanted wall below, you *can* lean over and touch your toes without toppling. Complete the sketch to the right to show how.

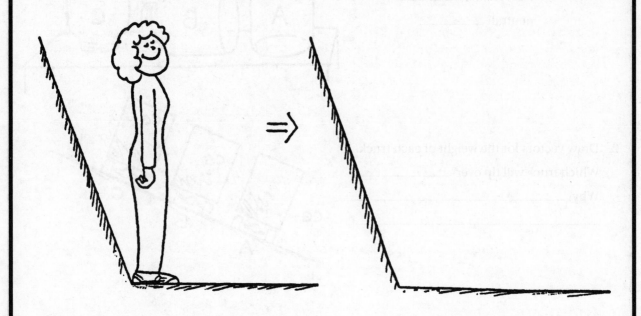

7. A person stands upright without difficulty. On each of the sketches below, draw the weight vector and show why the same person cannot stand on tiptoes against the wall.

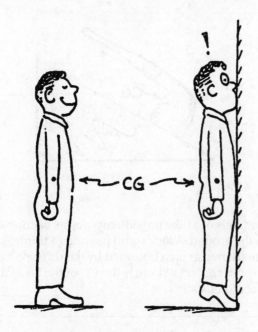

Concept-Development Practice Page **11-3**

Torques

1. Apply what you know about torques by making a mobile. Shown below are five horizontal arms with fixed 1- and 2-kg masses attached, and four hangers with ends that fit in the loops of the arms, lettered A through R. You are to figure where the loops should be attached so that when the whole system is suspended from the spring scale at the top, it will hang as a proper mobile, with its arms suspended horizontally. This is best done by working from the bottom upward. Circle the loops where the hangers should be attached. When the mobile is complete, how many kilograms will be indicated on the scale? (Assume the horizontal struts and connecting hooks are practically massless compared to the 1- and 2-kg masses.) On a separate sheet of paper, make a sketch of your completed mobile.

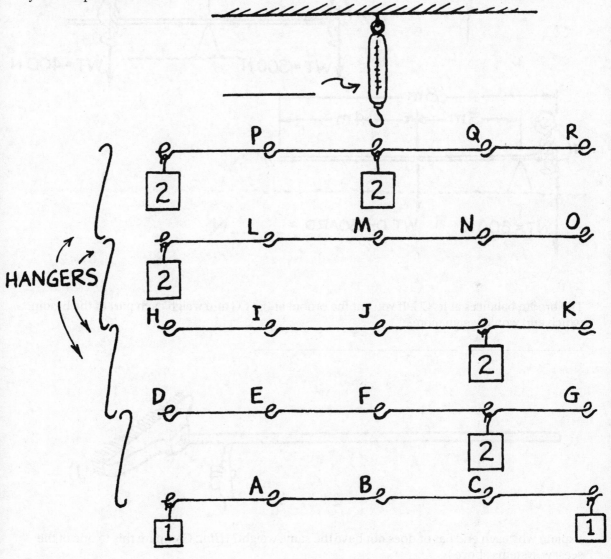

2. Complete the data for the three seesaws in equilibrium.

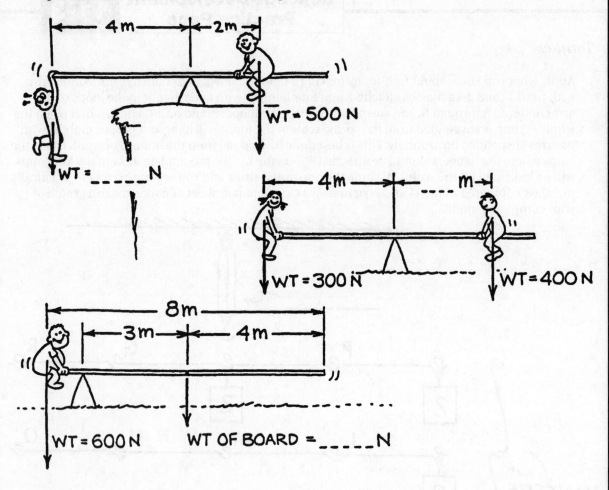

3. The broom balances at its CG. If you cut the broom at the CG and weigh each part of the broom, which end would weigh more?

_____

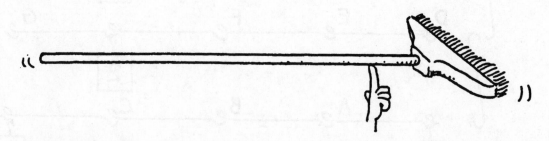

Explain why each end has or does not have the same weight? (*Hint*: Compare this to one of the seesaw systems above.)

_____

_____

CONCEPTUAL PHYSICS

Circular Motion

1. Most energy of train systems is used in starting and stopping. The *rotating train platform* design saves energy, for people can board or leave a train while the train is still moving. Study the sketch and convince yourself that this is true. The small circular platform in the middle is stationary, and is connected to a stationary stairway.

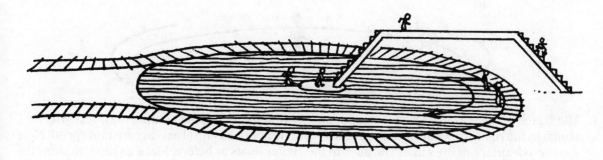

   a. If there is to be no relative motion between the train and the edge of the platform, how fast must the train move compared to the rim speed of the rotating platform?

   _____

   b. Why is the stairway located at the center of the platform?

   _____

2. The design below shows a train that makes round trips from Station A to Station B in a continuous loop.

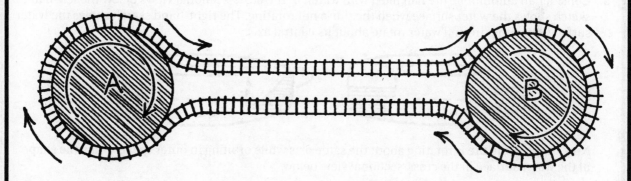

   a. How is the size of the round platform and train speed related to the amount of time that passengers have for boarding?

   _____

   _____

   b. Why would this rotating platform be impractical for high-speed trains?

   _____

   _____

CONCEPTUAL PHYSICS

3. Here are some people standing on a giant rotating platform in a fun house. In the view shown, the platform is not rotating and the people stand at rest.

When the platform rotates, the person in the middle stands as before. The person at the edge must lean inward as shown. Make a sketch of the missing people to show how they must lean in comparison.

4. The sketch at the left shows a stationary container of water and some floating toy ducks. The sketch at the right shows the same container rotating about a central axis at constant speed. Note the curved surface of the water. The duck in the center floats as before. Make a sketch to show the orientation of the other two ducks with respect to the water surface.

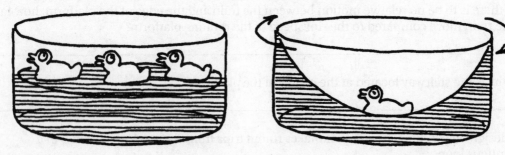

5. Consider an automobile tire half filled with water. In the cross-sectional views below the left-hand sketch shows the water surface when the tire is not rotating. The right-hand sketch shows the water surface when the tire and water rotate about its central axis.

Now suppose the tire is rotating about the same axis while orbiting in outer space. Draw the shape of the water surface in the cross-sectional view below.

In your mind, scale up the rotating tire model to a rotating space habitat orbiting in space. If the space habitat were half filled with water, could inhabitants float on the surface as they do here on Earth? Discuss this with your classmates.

Concept-Development Practice Page 12-2

Simulated Gravity and Frames of Reference

Susie Spacewalker and Bob Biker are in outer space. Bob experiences Earth-normal gravity in a rotating habitat, where centripetal force on his feet provides a normal support force that feels like weight. Suzie hovers outside in a weightless condition, motionless relative to the stars and the center of mass of the habitat.

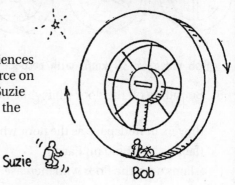

Suzie

Bob

1. Suzie sees Bob rotating clockwise in a circular path at a linear speed of 30 km/h. Suzie and Bob are facing each other, and from Bob's point of view, he is at rest and he sees Suzie moving

   (clockwise) (counterclockwise).

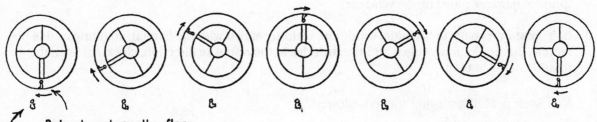

Bob at rest on the floor

Suzie hovering in space

2. The rotating habitat seems like home to Bob—until he rides his bicycle. When he rides in the opposite direction as the habitat rotates, Suzie sees him moving (faster) (slower).

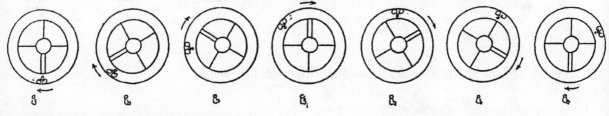

Bob rides counterclockwise

3. As Bob's bicycle speedometer reading increases, his rotational speed

   (decreases) (remains unchanged) (increases) and the normal force that feels like weight

   (decreases) (remains unchanged) (increases). So friction between the tires and the floor

   (decreases) (remains unchanged) (increases).

4. When Bob nevertheless gets his speed up to 30 km/h, as read on his bicycle speedometer, Suzie sees him

   (moving at 30 km/h) (motionless) (moving at 60 km/h).

CONCEPTUAL PHYSICS

thanx to Bob Becker

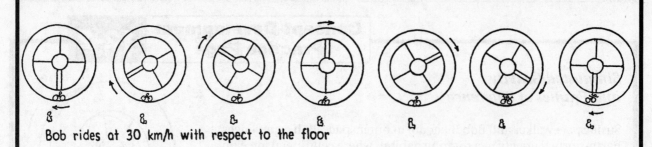

Bob rides at 30 km/h with respect to the floor

5. Bounding off the floor a bit while riding at 30 km/h, and neglecting wind effects, Bob

   (hovers in midspace as the floor whizzes by him at 30 km/h)
   (falls as he would on Earth)
   (slams onto the floor with increased force).

   and he finds himself

   (in the same frame of reference as Suzie)
   (as if he rode at 30 km/h on Earth's surface)
   (pressed harder against the bicycle seat).

6. Bob manuevers back to his initial condition, whirling at rest with the habitat, standing beside his bicycle. But not for long. Urged by Suzie, he rides in the opposite direction, clockwise with the rotation of the habitat.

   Now Suzie sees him moving (faster) (slower).

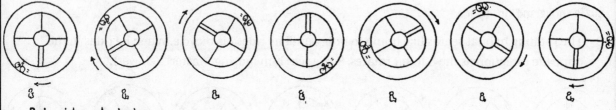

Bob rides clockwise

7. As Bob gains speed, the normal support force that feels like weight

   (decreases) (remains unchanged) (increases).

8. When Bob's speedometer reading gets up to 30 km/h, Suzie sees him

   (moving at 30 km/h) (motionless) (moving at 60 km/h)

   and Bob finds himself

   (weightless like Suzie)
   (just as if he rode at 30 km/h on Earth's surface)
   (pressed harder against the bicycle seat).

Next, Bob goes bowling. You decide whether the game depends on which direction the ball is rolled!

CONCEPTUAL PHYSICS

Inverse–Square Law

1. Paint spray travels radially away from the nozzle of the can in straight lines. Like gravity, the strength (intensity) of the spray obeys an inverse-square law. Complete the diagram by filling in the blank spaces.

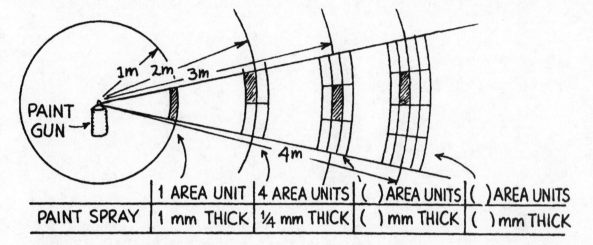

	1 AREA UNIT	4 AREA UNITS	( ) AREA UNITS	( ) AREA UNITS
PAINT SPRAY	1 mm THICK	¼ mm THICK	( ) mm THICK	( ) mm THICK

2. A small light source located 1 m in front of an opening of area 1 m² illuminates a wall behind. If the wall is 1 m behind the opening (2 m from the light source), the illuminated area covers 4 m². How many square meters will be illuminated if the wall is

5 m from the source? _____

10 m from the source? _____

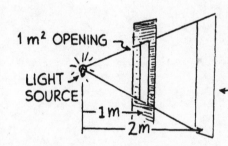

3. Hold your hands outstretched, one twice as far from your eyes as the other, and make a casual judgment as to which hand looks bigger. Most people see them to be about the same size, while many see the nearer hand as slightly bigger. Almost nobody upon casual inspection sees the nearer hand as four times as big. But because your vision depends upon an inverse-square law, the nearer hand should appear twice as tall and twice as wide, and there-fore occupy four times as much of your visual field, as the farther hand. Your belief that your hands are the same size is so strong that you likely overrule this information. Now if you overlap your hands slightly and view them with one eye closed, you'll see the nearer hand as clearly bigger. This raises an interesting question: What other illusions do you have that are not so easily checked?

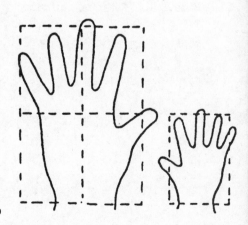

CONCEPTUAL PHYSICS

Force and Weight

1. An apple that has a mass of 0.1 kilogram has the same mass wherever it is. The amount of matter that makes up the apple

   (depends upon) (does not depend upon)

   the location of the apple. It has the same resistance to acceleration wherever it is—its inertia everywhere is

   (the same) (different).

   The weight of the apple is a different story. It may weigh exactly 1 N in San Francisco and slightly less in mile-high Denver, Colorado. On the surface of the moon the apple would weigh 1/6 N, and far out in outer space it may have almost no weight at all. The quantity that doesn't change with location is

   (mass) (weight),

   and the quantity that may change with location is its

   (mass) (weight).

   That's because

   (mass) (weight)

   is the force due to gravity on a body, and this force varies with distance. So weight is the force of gravity between two bodies, usually some small object in contact with Earth. When we refer to the

   (mass) (weight)

   of an object we are usually speaking of the gravitational force that attracts it to Earth.

   Fill in the blanks.

2. If we stand on a weighing scale and find that we are pulled toward Earth with a force of 500 N, then we weigh _____ N. Strictly speaking, we weigh _____ N relative to Earth. How much does Earth weigh? If we tip the scale upside down and repeat the weighing process, we can say that we and Earth are still pulled together with a force of _____ N, and therefore, relative to us, the whole 6,000,000,000,000,000,000,000,000-kg Earth weighs _____ N! Weight, unlike mass, is a relative quantity.

VIEW THE SAME FROM ANOTHER PERSPECTIVE!

DO YOU SEE WHY IT MAKES SENSE TO DISCUSS EARTH'S MASS, BUT NOT ITS WEIGHT?

We are pulled to Earth with a force of 500 N, so we weigh 500 N.

Earth is pulled toward us with a force of 500 N, so it weighs 500 N.

CONCEPTUAL PHYSICS

3. The spaceship is attracted to both the planet and the planet's moon. The planet has four times the mass of its moon. The force of attraction of the spaceship to the planet is shown by the vector.

a. Carefully sketch another vector to show the spaceship's attraction to the moon. Then use the parallelogram method of Chapter 3 and sketch the resultant force.

b. Determine the location between the planet and its moon where gravitational forces cancel. Make a sketch of the spaceship there.

4. Consider a planet of uniform density that has a straight tunnel from the North Pole through the center to the South Pole. At the surface of the planet, an object weighs 1 ton.

a. Fill in the gravitational force on the object when it is half way to the center, then at the center.

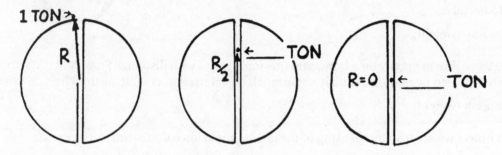

b. Describe the motion you would experience if you fell into the tunnel.

_____

5. Consider an object that weighs 1 ton at the surface of a planet, just before the planet gravitationally collapses. (The mass of the planet remains the same during collapse.)

a. Fill in the weights of the object on the planet's shrinking surface at the radial values shown.

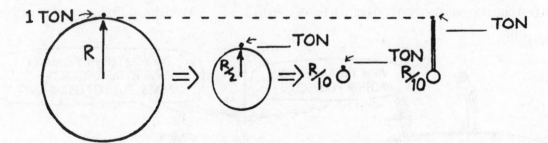

b. When the planet has collapsed to a tenth of its initial radius, a ladder is erected that puts the object as far from its center as the object was originally. Fill in its weight at this position.

CONCEPTUAL PHYSICS

Gravitational Interactions

The equation for the law of universal gravitation is

$$F = G \frac{m_1 m_2}{d^2}$$

where F is the attractive force between masses m_1 and m_2 separated by distance d. G is the universal gravitational constant (and relates G to the masses and distance as the constant π similarly relates the circumference of a circle to its diameter). By substituting changes in any of the variables into this equation, we can predict how the others change. For example, we can see how the force changes if we know how either or both of the masses change, or how the distance between their centers changes.

Suppose, for example, that one of the masses somehow is doubled. Then substituting $2m_1$ for m_1 in the equation gives

$$F_{new} = G \frac{2m_1 m_2}{d^2} = 2G \frac{m_1 m_2}{d^2} = 2F_{old}$$

So we see the force doubles also. Or suppose instead that the distance of separation is doubled. Then substituting $2d$ for d in the equation gives

$$F_{new} = G \frac{m_1 m_2}{(2d)^2} = G \frac{m_1 m_2}{4d^2} = \frac{1}{4} G \frac{m_1 m_2}{d^2} = \frac{1}{4} F_{old}$$

And we see the force is only 1/4 as much.

Use this method to solve the following problems. Write the equation and make the appropriate substitutions.

1. If both masses are doubled, what happens to the force?

2. If the masses are not changed, but the distance of separation is reduced to half the original distance, what happens to the force?

GRAVITY
:SIGH:

CONCEPTUAL PHYSICS

3. If the masses are not changed, but the distance of separation is reduced to one fourth the original distance, what happens to the force?

4. If both masses are doubled, and the distance of separation is doubled, show what happens to the force.

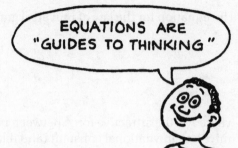

EQUATIONS ARE "GUIDES TO THINKING"

5. If one of the masses is doubled, the other remains unchanged, and the distance of separation is tripled, show what happens to the force.

6. Consider a pair of binary stars that pull on each other with a certain force. Would the force be larger or smaller if the mass of each star were three times as great when their distance apart is three times as far? Show what the new force will be compared to the first one.

CONCEPTUAL PHYSICS

Our Ocean Tides

1. Consider two equal-mass blobs of water, A and B, initially at rest in the moon's gravitational field. The vector shows the gravitational force of the moon on A.

   a. Draw a force vector on B due to the moon's gravity.

   b. Is the force on B more or less than the force on A? _____

   c. Why?_____

   d. The blobs accelerate toward the moon. Which has the greater acceleration? (A) (B)

   e. Because of the different accelerations, with time

   (A gets farther ahead of B) (A and B gain identical speeds) and the distance between A and B

   (increases) (stays the same) (decreases).

   f. If A and B were connected by a rubber band, with time the rubber band would

   (stretch) (not stretch).

   g. This (stretching) (non-stretching) is due to the (difference) (non-difference) in the moon's gravitational pulls.

   h. The two blobs will eventually crash into the moon. To orbit around the moon instead of crashing into it, the blobs should move

   (away from the moon) (tangentially).   Then their accelerations will consist of changes in (speed) (direction).

2. Now consider the same two blobs located on opposite sides of Earth.

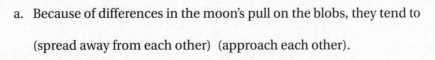

   a. Because of differences in the moon's pull on the blobs, they tend to

   (spread away from each other) (approach each other).

   b. Does this spreading produce ocean tides? (Yes) (No)

   c. If Earth and moon were closer, gravitational force between them would be (more) (the same) (less), and the difference in gravitational forces on the near and far parts of the ocean would be (more) (the same) (less).

   d. Because Earth's orbit about the sun is slightly elliptical, Earth and sun are closer in December than in June. Taking the sun's tidal force into account, on a world average, ocean tides are greater in (December) (June) (no difference).

CONCEPTUAL PHYSICS

**Concept-Development
Practice Page** **14-1**

Satellite Motion

1. Figure A shows "Newton's Mountain," so high that its top is above the drag of the atmosphere. The cannonball is fired and hits the ground as shown.

   a. Draw the path the cannonball might take if it were fired a little bit faster.

   b. Repeat for a still greater speed, but still less than 8 km/s.

   c. Draw the orbital path it would take if its speed were 8 km/s.

   d. What is the shape of the 8 km/s curve?
   _____

   e. What would be the shape of the orbital path if the cannonball were fired at a speed of about 9 km/s?
   _____

Figure A

2. Figure B shows a satellite in circular orbit.

   a. At each of the four positions draw a vector that represents the gravitational *force* exerted on the satellite.

   b. Label the force vectors **F**.

   c. Draw at each position a vector to represent the *velocity* of the satellite at that position, and label it **v**.

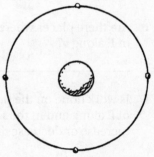

Figure B

   d. Are all four **F** vectors the same length? Why or why not?
   _____

   e. Are all four **v** vectors the same length? Why or why not?
   _____

   f. What is the angle between your **F** and **v** vectors? _____

   g. Is there any component of **F** along **v**? _____

   h. What does this tell you about the work the force of gravity does on the satellite?
   _____

   i. Does the KE of the satellite in Figure B remain constant, or does it vary?
   _____

   j. Does the PE of the satellite remain constant, or does it vary?
   _____

CONCEPTUAL PHYSICS

3. Figure C shows a satellite in elliptical orbit.

a. Repeat the procedure you used for the circular orbit, drawing vectors **F** and **v** for each position, including proper labeling. Show equal magnitudes with equal lengths, and greater magnitudes with greater lengths, but don't bother making the scale accurate.

b. Are your vectors **F** all the same magnitude? Why or why not?

_____

_____

c. Are your vectors **v** all the same magnitude? Why or why not?

_____

_____

_____

_____

d. Is the angle between vectors **F** and **v** everywhere the same, or does it vary?

_____

e. Are there places where there is a component of **F** along **v**?

_____

f. Is work done on the satellite when there is a component of **F** along and in the same direction of **v** and if so, does this increase or decrease the KE of the satellite?

_____

Figure C

g. When there is a component of **F** along and opposite to the direction of **v**, does this increase or decrease the KE of the satellite?

_____

_____

_____

h. What can you say about the sum KE + PE along the orbit?

_____

_____

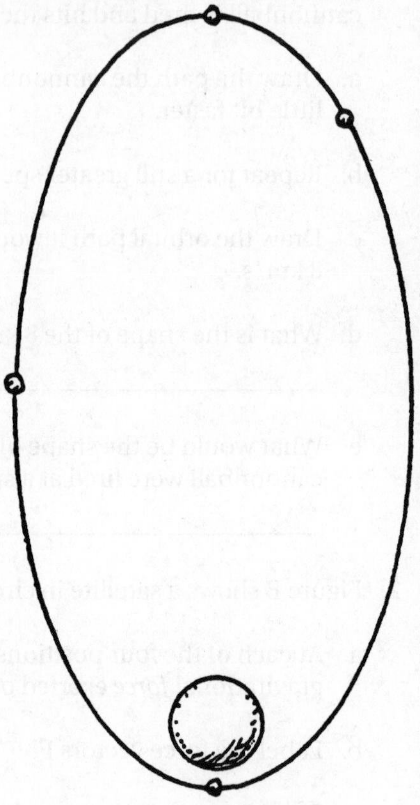

CONCEPTUAL PHYSICS

The Twin Trip

This is about identical twins, one an astronaut who takes a high-speed round-trip journey while the other twin stays home on Earth. The traveling twin returns younger than the stay-at-home twin. How much younger depends on the relative speeds involved. If the traveling twin maintains a speed of 0.5c for 1 year (according to clocks aboard the spaceship), 1.15 years elapse on Earth. For a speed of 0.87c, 2 years elapse on Earth. At 0.995c, 10 Earth years pass in one spaceship year; the traveling twin ages a single year while the stay-at-home twin ages 10 years.

This exercise will show that from the frames of reference of both the Earthbound twin and traveling twin, the Earthbound twin ages more.

Case 1: No Motion First, consider a spaceship hovering at rest relative to a distant planet (left). Suppose the spaceship sends regularly-spaced brief flashes of light to the planet. The light flashes encounter a receiver on the planet a slight time later at speed c. Since there is no relative motion between sender and receiver, successive flashes are received as frequently as they are sent. We'll suppose that a flash is sent from the ship every 6 minutes; after a slight delay, the receiver receives a flash every 6 minutes. Nothing is unusual because no motion is involved.

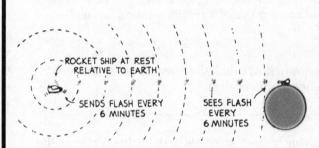

ROCKET SHIP AT REST RELATIVE TO EARTH

SENDS FLASH EVERY 6 MINUTES

SEES FLASH EVERY 6 MINUTES

Case 2: Motion For motion the situation is quite different. Although the speed of the flashes is c, regardless of motion, how *frequently* the flashes are seen depends on relative motion. When the ship approaches the receiver, the receiver sees the flashes more frequently. This makes sense because each succeeding flash has less distance to travel as the ship gets closer to the receiver. Flashes are "crowded together" and are seen more frequently. Flashes sent at 6-minute intervals are seen less than 6 minutes apart. We'll suppose the ship is traveling fast enough for the flashes to be seen twice as frequently, at 3-minute intervals (right). This is the Doppler effect (Chapter 25) for light.

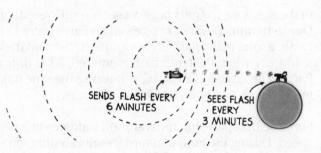

SENDS FLASH EVERY 6 MINUTES

SEES FLASH EVERY 3 MINUTES

CONCEPTUAL PHYSICS

Moving away from the receiver stretches the flashes apart and they are seen less frequently. If the ship recedes from the receiver at the same speed and still emits flashes at 6-minute intervals, these flashes are seen by the receiver as stretched to 12-minute intervals. Put another way, they are seen half as frequently, that is, one flash each 12 minutes (right). This makes sense because each succeeding flash has a longer distance to travel as the ship gets farther away from the receiver.

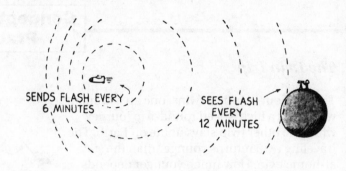

Note the effect of moving away is the opposite of moving closer to the receiver. Although flashes are received twice as frequently when the ship is approaching (6-minute flash intervals are seen every 3 minutes), they're received half as frequently when receding (6-minute flash intervals are seen every 12 minutes).

The light flashes make up a light clock. Any reliable clock would show that 6-minute intervals in the spaceship appear 12 minutes apart when the spaceship recedes and only 3 minutes apart when the ship approaches (that's *twice* as long apart when receding, *half* as long apart when approaching).

1. If the spaceship travels for 1 hour and emits a flash each 6 minutes, how many flashes will be emitted? _____

2. The ship sends equally-spaced 6-minute flashes while approaching a receiver. Will these flashes be received equally spaced if the ship approaches at constant velocity while sending flashes?

   _____

3. If the receiver sees these flashes at 3-minute intervals, how much time occurs between receiving the first and the last flash (in the frame of reference of the receiver)?

   _____

Case 3: The Twins Let's apply this doubling and halving of flash intervals to the twins. Suppose the traveling twin recedes from the Earthbound twin at the same high speed for 1 hour and then quickly turns around and returns in 1 hour. The traveling twin takes a round trip of 2 hours, according to clocks aboard the spaceship. But the time for this round trip will be different as seen in the Earth frame of reference.

In the figure on the next page we see the ship receding from Earth, emitting a flash each 6 minutes. Due to motion, flashes are received on Earth every 12 minutes. During the hour of going away from Earth, a total of ten flashes are emitted. If the ship departs from Earth at noon, clocks aboard the ship read 1 P.M. when the tenth flash is emitted. What time will it be on Earth when this tenth flash reaches Earth? The answer is 2 P.M. Why? Because the time it takes Earth to receive 10 flashes at 12-minute intervals is 10×12 min = 120 min = 2 hours.

Suppose the spaceship turns around suddenly in a negligibly short time and returns at the same high speed. During the hour of return it emits another ten flashes at 6-minute intervals. These flashes are received every 3 minutes on Earth, so all ten flashes arrive in 30 minutes. A clock on Earth will read 2:30 P.M. when the spaceship completes its 2-hour trip. We see that the Earthbound twin has aged 1/2 hour more than the twin aboard the spaceship!

CONCEPTUAL PHYSICS

The Twin Trip—continued

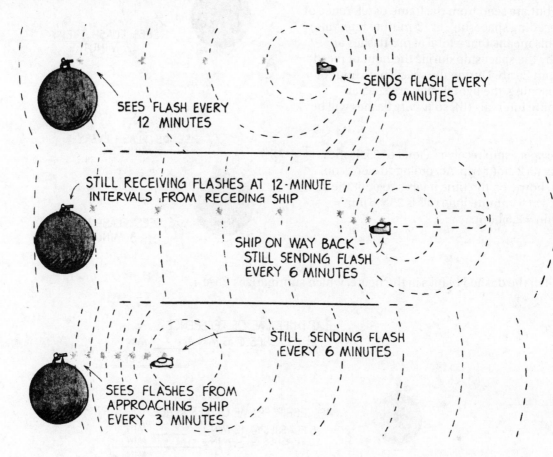

SEES FLASH EVERY
12 MINUTES

SENDS FLASH EVERY
6 MINUTES

STILL RECEIVING FLASHES AT 12-MINUTE
INTERVALS FROM RECEDING SHIP

SHIP ON WAY BACK -
STILL SENDING FLASH
EVERY 6 MINUTES

STILL SENDING FLASH
EVERY 6 MINUTES

SEES FLASHES FROM
APPROACHING SHIP
EVERY 3 MINUTES

4. Complete the figure below, which summarizes Case 3, by filling in the blanks.

EARTH FRAME OF REFERENCE:
10 FLASHES @ 12 MIN = ____ MIN
10 FLASHES @ 3 MIN = ____ MIN
          ____ MIN
          ____ HOURS

SPACESHIP FRAME OF REFERENCE:
20 FLASHES @ 6 MIN = ____ MIN
          ____ HOURS

CONCEPTUAL PHYSICS

Case 4: Sending and Receiving Twins Interchanged Let's switch sender and receiver and see if the result is the same in both frames of reference. Flashes are emitted from Earth at regularly spaced 6-minute intervals in Earth time, but are seen from the frame of reference of the receding spaceship, at 12-minute intervals (A). This means that a total of *five* flashes are seen by the spaceship during the hour of receding from Earth. During the spaceship's hour of approaching, the light flashes are seen at 3-minute intervals (B), so *twenty* flashes will be seen.

So the spaceship receives a total of 25 flashes during its 2-hour trip. According to clocks on Earth, however, the time it takes to emit the 25 flashes at 6-minute intervals is 25 × 6 min = 150 min = 2.5 hours.

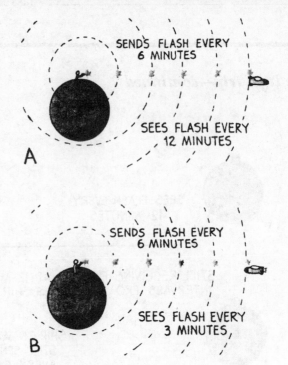

5. Fill in the dashed blanks in the figure, which summarizes Case 4.

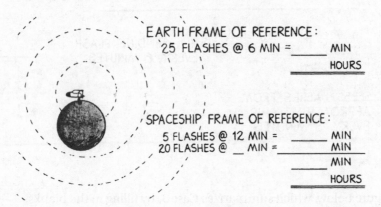

EARTH FRAME OF REFERENCE:
25 FLASHES @ 6 MIN = _____ MIN
_____ HOURS

SPACESHIP FRAME OF REFERENCE:
5 FLASHES @ 12 MIN = _____ MIN
20 FLASHES @ __ MIN = _____ MIN
_____ MIN
_____ HOURS

Conclusion So both twins agree on the same results, with no dispute as to who ages more. The key factor is that while the stay-at-home twin remains in a single reference frame, the traveling twin experiences two different frames of reference, separated by the acceleration of the spaceship in turning around. So the spaceship experiences two different realms of time, while Earth-bound observers experience a still different but single realm of time. The twins can meet again at the same location in space only at the expense of time.

6. The twin example is often called the twin "paradox" because of the following reasoning:

Since motion is relative, the spaceship can be regarded at rest while Earth moves, in which

case the twin on the spaceship ages more. Is the situation symmetrical; that is, do both twins

occupy the same realm of time? _____ What event separates the _____ realms of time

for the traveling twin? _____ In terms of

symmetry, is this twin-paradox reasoning correct or incorrect? _____ Briefly, why?

CONCEPTUAL PHYSICS

Concept-Development Practice Page **15-2**

Space and Time

The Twin-Trip compares the times experienced by a traveling twin and a stay-at-home twin. The 2-hour trip experienced by the traveling twin is observed to take 2.5 hours from a frame of reference on Earth, as evidenced by the sending and receiving of regularly-spaced flashes of light. The 6-minute-interval flashes emitted by the spaceship are seen from Earth at 12-minute intervals when the spaceship is leaving Earth, and at 3-minute intervals when the spaceship is approaching Earth. Fill in the readings on the spaceship clock below for each flash emitted, and on the Earth clock for each flash received.

SHIP LEAVING EARTH

FLASH	TIME ON ROCKET WHEN FLASH SENT	TIME ON EARTH WHEN FLASH SEEN
0	12:00	12:00
1	12:06	
2		
3		
4		
5		
6		
7		
8		
9		
10		

SHIP APPROACHING EARTH

FLASH	TIME ON ROCKET WHEN FLASH SENT	TIME ON EARTH WHEN FLASH SEEN
11		
12		
13		
14		
15		
16		
17		
18		
19		
20		

The fact that the clocks read differently when each is in a different realm of spacetime is a consequence of differences in

(the clock mechanisms) (time itself).

CONCEPTUAL PHYSICS

Length, Momentum, and Energy

1. Pretend we are on a space mission to Jupiter. Our instruments detect an identical sister space station, Alpha Alberta, moving away from us at 80% of the speed of light. Our instruments reveal that, compared to our station,

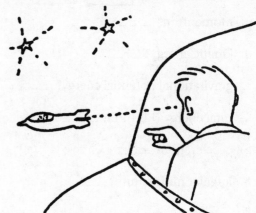

   a. clocks and events on Alpha Alberta are

      (slow) (fast) (the same).

   b. the length of Alpha Alberta in its direction of motion appears

      (shorter) (longer) (the same).

   c. the momentum of Alpha Alberta is

      (more) (less) (the same).

   Occupants on Alpha Alberta are making measurements of us. They observe that, compared to their station,

   d. clocks and events on our space station are

      (slow) (fast) (the same).

   e. the length of our space station is

      (shorter) (longer) (the same).

   f. our momentum is

      (more) (less) (the same).

2. A gram of water has a volume of 1 cubic centimeter, about the size of a sugar cube. A gram of iron has a smaller volume, about the size of a pea, and a gram of platinum is even smaller, about the size of a small raisin. In a gram of any kind of matter is an equivalent vast amount of rest energy. We can see how much energy a gram of matter is equal to in joules from the celebrated equation $E = mc^2$, where $m = 1 \text{ g} = 10^{-3} \text{ kg}$, and $c = 3 \times 10^8 \text{ m/s}$. Then

   $$E = mc^2 = (10^{-3} \text{ kg})(3 \times 10^8 \text{ m/s})^2 = 9 \times 10^{13} \text{ J}$$

   In comparison, one barrel of crude oil when burned yields 6×10^9 J. According to this data, is the statement by the man at the right an overestimate, an underestimate, or accurate? Defend your answer.

   BURN 15,000 BARRELS OF OIL AND YOU EQUAL THE ENERGY EQUIVALENT OF ANY GRAM OF MATTER?

   _____

   _____

CONCEPTUAL PHYSICS

1. The sketch shows the elliptical path described by a satellite about Earth. In which of the marked positions, A – D, (put S for "same everywhere") does the satellite experience the maximum

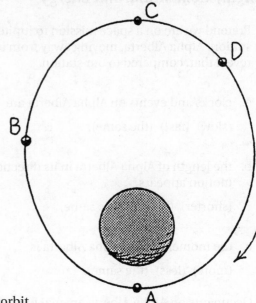

   a. gravitational force? _____

   b. speed? _____

   c. momentum? _____

   d. kinetic energy? _____

   e. gravitational potential energy? _____

   f. total energy (KE + PE)? _____

   g. acceleration? _____

   h. angular momentum? _____

2. Answer the above questions for a satellite in circular orbit.

   a. _____   b. _____   c. _____   d. _____   e. _____   f. _____   g. _____   h. _____

3. In which position(s) is there momentarily no work being done on the satellite by the force of gravity? Why?

   _____

4. Work changes energy. Let the equation for work, $W = Fd$, guide your thinking on these: Defend your answers in terms of $W = Fd$.

   a. In which position will a several-minutes thrust of rocket engines pushing the satellite forward do the most work on the satellite and give it the greatest change in kinetic energy? (*Hint:* Think about where the most distance will be traveled during the application of a several-minutes thrust.)

   _____

   b. In which position will a several-minutes thrust of rocket engines pushing the satellite forward do the least work on the satellite and give it the least boost in kinetic energy?

   _____

   c. In which position will a several-minutes thrust of a retro-rocket (pushing opposite to the satellite's direction of motion) do the most work on the satellite and change its kinetic energy the most?

   _____

CONCEPTUAL PHYSICS

**Concept-Development
Practice Page** 17-1

The Atomic Nature of Matter

ATOMS ARE CLASSIFIED BY THEIR ATOMIC NUMBER, WHICH IS THE SAME AS THE NUMBER OF _____ IN THE NUCLEUS.

TO CHANGE THE ATOMS OF ONE ELEMENT INTO THOSE OF ANOTHER, _____ MUST BE ADDED OR SUBTRACTED!

Use the periodic table on page 336 of your text to help you answer the following questions.

1. When the atomic nuclei of hydrogen and lithium are squashed together (nuclear fusion) the element that is produced is

   _____

2. When the atomic nuclei of a pair of lithium nuclei are fused, the element produced is

   _____

3. When the atomic nuclei of a pair of aluminum nuclei are fused, the element produced is

   _____

4. When the nucleus of a nitrogen atom absorbs a proton, the resulting element is

   _____

5. What element is produced when a gold nucleus gains a proton?

   _____

6. Which results in the more valuable product – *adding* or *subtracting* protons from gold nuclei?

   _____

   _____

7. What element is produced when a uranium nucleus ejects an elementary particle composed of two protons and two neutrons?

   _____

8. If a uranium nucleus breaks into two pieces (nuclear fission) and one of the pieces is zirconium (atomic number 40), the other piece is the element

   _____

9. Which has more mass, a nitrogen molecule (N_2) or an oxygen molecule (O_2)?

   _____

I LIKE THE WAY YOUR ATOMS ARE PUT TOGETHER!

SIGH

10. Which has the greater number of atoms, a gram of helium or a gram of neon?

   _____

CONCEPTUAL PHYSICS

Subatomic Particles

Three fundamental particles of the atom are the _____, _____, and _____. At the center of each atom lies the atomic _____ which consists of _____ and _____. The atomic number refers to the number of _____ in the nucleus. All atoms of the same element have the same number of _____, hence, the same atomic number.

Isotopes are atoms that have the same number of _____ but a different number of _____. An isotope is identified by its atomic mass number, which is the total number of _____ and _____ in the nucleus. A carbon isotope that has 6 _____ and _____ is identified as carbon-12, where 12 is the atomic mass number. A carbon isotope having 6 _____ and 8 _____, on the other hand is carbon-14.

1. Complete the table.

ISOTOPE	ELECTRONS	NUMBER OF PROTONS	NEUTRONS
Hydrogen-1	1		
Chlorine-36		17	
Nitrogen-14			7
Potassium-40	19		
Arsenic-75		33	
Gold-197			118

2. Which has more mass, a lead atom or a uranium atom?

   _____

3. Which has a greater number of atoms, a gram of lead or a gram of uranium?

   _____

Of every 200 atoms in our bodies, 126 are hydrogen, 51 are oxygen, and just 19 are carbon. In addition to carbon we need iron to manufacture hemoglobin, cobalt for the creation of vitamin B-12, potassium and a little sodium for our nerves, and molybdenum, manganese, and vanadium to keep our enzymes purring. Ah, we'd be nothing without atoms!

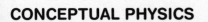

**Concept-Development
Practice Page**   **18-1**

Scaling Squares

1. ☐   If you have square 1 cm on each side, what is its area? _____ cm²

A SQUARE OF SIDE ℓ HAS AN AREA ℓ^2

2. ☐   If you have a square 2 cm on each side, what is its area? _____ cm²

3. Consider a square piece of pizza, 10 cm × 10 cm. Another piece of pizza measures 20 cm × 20 cm. How does the area of the larger pizza compare?

_____

4. If you have a square 4 cm on each side, what is its area? _____ cm²

5. If you have a square 10 cm on each side, what is its area? _____ cm²

6. If you double each side of a square, how many times as large does its area become?

_____

7. If you triple each side of a square, how many times as large does its area become?

_____

8. *True or false*: If the side of a square is increased by a certain factor, say 5, then the area increases by the *square* of the factor, in this case 5² (or 25). _____

So, if you scale up the side of a square by a factor of 10, its area will increase by a factor of _____ or _____.

WHEN YOU DOUBLE THE SIDE OF A SQUARE, YOU GET _____ TIMES THE AREA

AND IF YOU TRIPLE THE SIDE OF A SQUARE YOU GET _____ TIMES THE AREA

IN GENERAL, IF YOU X THE SIDE OF A SQUARE, YOU X² THE AREA!

CONCEPTUAL PHYSICS

Scaling Circles

1. Complete the table.

CIRCLES		
RADIUS	CIRCUMFERENCE	AREA
1 cm	$2\pi(1cm) = 2\pi$ cm	$\pi(1cm)^2 = \pi\,cm^2$
2 cm		
3 cm		
10 cm		

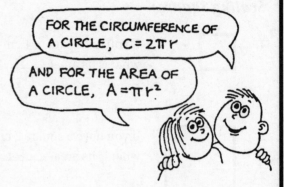

FOR THE CIRCUMFERENCE OF A CIRCLE, $C = 2\pi r$

AND FOR THE AREA OF A CIRCLE, $A = \pi r^2$

2. From your completed table, when the radius of a circle is doubled, its area increases by a factor of _____. When the radius is increased by a factor of 10, the area increases by a factor of _____.

3. Consider a round pizza that costs $2.00. Another pizza of the same thickness has twice the diameter. How much should the larger pizza cost?

   _____

4. *True or false*: If the radius of a circle is increased by a certain factor, say 5, then the area increases by the *square* of the factor, in this case 5^2 or 25. _____

   So if you scale up the radius of a circle by a factor of 10, its area will increase by a factor of _____.

5. *Application:* Suppose you raise chickens and spend $50 to buy wire for a chicken pen. To hold the most chickens inside, you should make the shape of the pen

   (square) (circular) (either, for both provide the same area).

CONCEPTUAL PHYSICS

Concept-Development Practice Page | 18-2

Scaling Cubes

1. Consider a cube, say 1 cm × 1 cm × 1 cm (about the size of a sugar cube). Its volume is 1 cm^3. The surface area of one of its faces is 1 cm^2. This is also the area of any cross section (a slice through the cube that is parallel to any of its faces). The total surface area of the cube is 6 cm^2, because it has 6 faces (4 sides and top and bottom; count them).

    Now consider a second cube, scaled up by a factor of 2 so it is 2 cm × 2 cm × 2 cm.

    a. What is the total surface areas of each cube?

        1st cube _____ cm^2; 2nd cube _____ cm^2

    b. How many times more is the total surface area of the second cube compared to that of the first?

        _____

    c. What are the volumes of the cubes?

        1st cube _____ cm^3; 2nd cube _____ cm^3

    d. How many times more is the volume of the second cube compared to that of the first?

        _____

    e. Compare the surface-area-to-volume ratio for

        1st cube: $\dfrac{\text{surface area}}{\text{volume}}$ = _____   2nd cube: $\dfrac{\text{surface area}}{\text{volume}}$ = _____

2. As the size of a cube (or object of any shape) increases, the ratio of surface area to volume decreases. This means that the gain in surface area is proportionally less than the gain in volume. (Area gains only as the *square* of the increase, while volume gains as the *cube* of the increase.) Apply this relationship and good thinking to explain the following:

    a. Why does a cup of coffee cool faster than the pot from which it is poured? Or, if you want your coffee to stay warm, should you pour it into a cup or leave it in the pot? Explain.

        _____

        _____

    b. Chickens, Cornish game hens, and turkeys have approximately the same body shape. If you had two birds, one with a body twice as wide, twice as thick, and twice as long, how would you expect their weights to compare? How about the amounts of skin?

        _____

        _____

CONCEPTUAL PHYSICS

Scaling Solids

1. a. Consider a pair of cubes, each 1 cm on a side. The volume
   of each cube is _____ cm³, so the total volume of both cubes
   is _____ cm³. The total surface area of each cube is _____ cm²,
   so the total surface area of both cubes is _____ cm².

    b. If the two cubes are glued together, to make a double cube,
      the total volume is _____ cm³ and the total exposed surface
      area is _____ cm².

2. The sketch to the right is a scaled-up version of the small double cube. It is scaled up by a factor of
   2 (twice as wide, twice as thick, and twice as tall).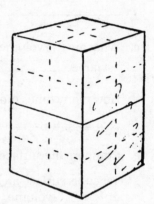

   a. Its volume is _____ cm³.

   b. Its total surface area is _____ cm².

   c. Which has the greater surface-area-to-volume ratio, the small or
      the scaled-up double cube?

      _____

      _____

3. Scale up the double cube of Question 2 by a factor of 3 (three times
   as tall and three times as wide both ways). Make a sketch of it in the
   space at the right.

   a. Its volume is _____ cm³.

   b. Its total surface area is _____ cm².

   c. Which of the three versions of the double cube has the
      most surface area? _____

   d. Which has the most surface area compared to its volume?

      _____
   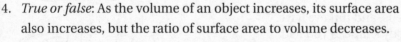
   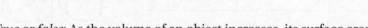
   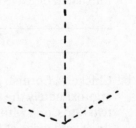

4. *True or false*: As the volume of an object increases, its surface area
   also increases, but the ratio of surface area to volume decreases.

   _____

5. The effects of scaling are good for some creatures and bad for
   others. Write either good (G) or bad (B) for each of the following:

   a. An insect falling from a tall tree _____   b. An elephant falling from the same tree _____

   c. A small fish trying to flee a big fish _____   d. A big fish chasing a small fish _____

   e. An insect that falls in the water _____   f. A hungry sparrow _____

**Concept-Development
Practice Page** 19-1

Archimedes' Principle I

1. Consider a balloon filled with 1 liter of water (1000 cm³) in equilibrium in a container of water, as shown in Figure 1.

   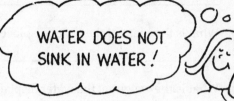

   a. What is the mass of the 1 liter of water?

   _____

   b. What is the weight of the 1 liter of water?

   _____

   c. What is the weight of water displaced by the balloon?

   _____

   d. What is the buoyant force on the balloon?

   _____

   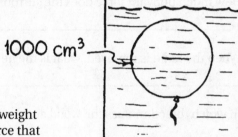

   e. Sketch a pair of vectors in Figure 1: one for the weight of the balloon and the other for the buoyant force that acts on it. How do the size and directions of your vectors compare?

   _____

   Figure 1

2. As a thought experiment, pretend we could remove the water from the balloon but still have it remain the same size of 1 liter. Then inside the balloon is a vacuum.

   a. What is the mass of the liter of nothing?

   _____

   b. What is the weight of the liter of nothing?

   _____

   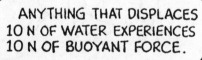

   c. What is the weight of water displaced by the massless balloon?

   _____

   d. What is the buoyant force on the massless balloon?

   _____

   e. In which direction would the massless balloon be accelerated?

   _____

CONCEPTUAL PHYSICS

3. Assume the balloon is replaced by a 0.5-kilogram piece of wood that has exactly the same volume (1000 cm³), as shown in Figure 2. The wood is held in the same submerged position beneath the surface of the water.

1000 cm³ →

Figure 2

a. What volume of water is displaced by the wood?

_____

b. What is the mass of the water displaced by the wood?

_____

c. What is the weight of the water displaced by the wood?

_____

d. How much buoyant force does the surrounding water exert on the wood?

_____

e. When the hand is removed, what is the net force on the wood?

_____

f. In which direction does the wood accelerate when released? _____

THE BUOYANT FORCE ON A SUBMERGED OBJECT EQUALS THE WEIGHT OF WATER DISPLACED

... NOT THE WEIGHT OF THE OBJECT ITSELF!

... UNLESS IT IS FLOATING!

4. Repeat parts (a) through (f) in the previous question for a 5-kg rock that has the same volume (1000 cm³), as shown in Figure 3. Assume the rock is suspended by a string in the container of water.

a. _____

b. _____

c. _____

d. _____

e. _____

f. _____

Figure 3

1000 cm³

WHEN THE WEIGHT OF AN OBJECT IS GREATER THAN THE BUOYANT FORCE EXERTED ON IT, IT SINKS!

CONCEPTUAL PHYSICS

**Concept-Development
Practice Page** | **19-2**

Archimedes' Principle II

1. The water lines for the first three cases are shown. Sketch in the appropriate water lines for cases (d) and (e), and make up your own for case (f).

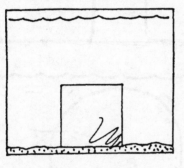

a. DENSER THAN WATER

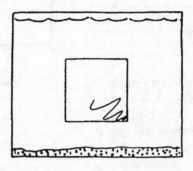

b. SAME DENSITY AS WATER

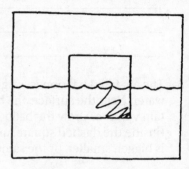

c. 1/2 AS DENSE AS WATER

d. 1/4 AS DENSE AS WATER

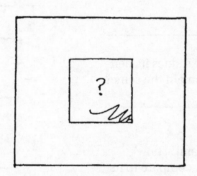

e. 3/4 AS DENSE AS WATER

f. _____ AS DENSE AS WATER

2. If the weight of a ship is 100 million N, then the water it displaces weighs _____.

   If cargo weighing 1000 N is put on board then the ship will sink down until an extra

   _____ of water is displaced.

3. The first two sketches below show the water line for an empty and a loaded ship. Draw in the appropriate water line for the third sketch.

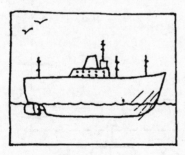

a. SHIP EMPTY

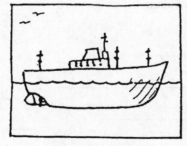

b. SHIP LOADED WITH
50 TONS OF IRON

c. SHIP LOADED WITH
50 TONS OF INSULATION

CONCEPTUAL PHYSICS

4. Here is a glass of ice water with an ice cube floating in it. Draw the water line after the ice cube melts. (Will the water line rise, fall, or remain the same?)

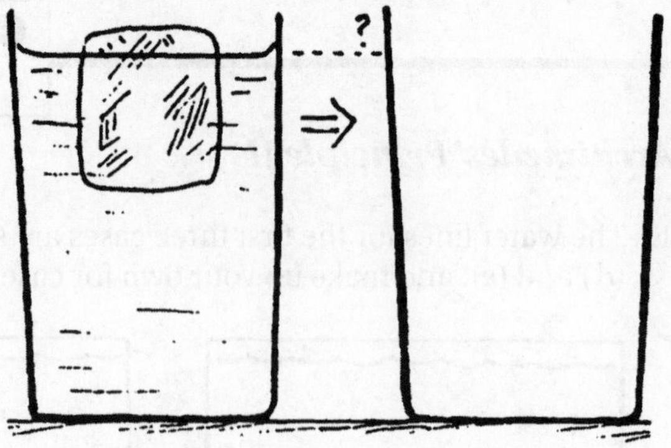

_____

_____

_____

_____

5. The air-filled balloon is weighted so it sinks in water. Near the surface, the balloon has a certain volume. Draw the balloon at the bottom (inside the dashed square) and show whether it is bigger, smaller, or the same size.

   a. Since the weighted balloon sinks, how does its overall density compare to the density of water?

   _____

   b. As the weighted balloon sinks, does its density increase, decrease, or remain the same?

   _____

   c. Since the weighted balloon sinks, how does the buoyant force on it compare to its weight?

   _____

   d. As the weighted balloon sinks deeper, does the buoyant force on it increase, decrease, or remain the same?

   _____

6. What would be your answers to Questions (a), (b), (c), and (d), for a rock instead of an air-filled balloon?

   a. _____

   b. _____

   c. _____

   d. _____

CONCEPTUAL PHYSICS

Concept-Development Practice Page 20-1

Syringes and Vacuum Pumps

The old fashioned farm-type pump shown in Figure 20.9 in your text is a *lift pump* that operates by atmospheric pressure. Its operation is similar to that of a common *syringe* (the device that holds the needle your doctor or dentist uses, or the gadget inside a toy water pistol).

1. The nozzle of the syringe is held beneath the surface of water in Figure A. When the piston is pulled up, water fills the nozzle and the chamber under the piston.

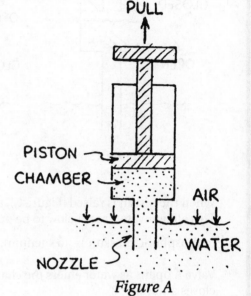

Figure A

a. What forces water into the nozzle and chamber?

_____

_____

b. When the syringe is removed from the water and held in the air, the water doesn't leak out. Why?

_____

_____

c. Would water leak out if air leaked past the piston? Explain briefly.

_____

_____

_____

d. What happens if the piston is pushed down? (Do you see how water pistols work?)

_____

_____

_____

2. A lift pump is like a syringe with two valves. Valve A is like a little door that lets water come up but will not let water go down again. Valve B is in the piston; it also lets water come up but not down again. In Figure B, both valves are closed and there are no regions of reduced air pressure.

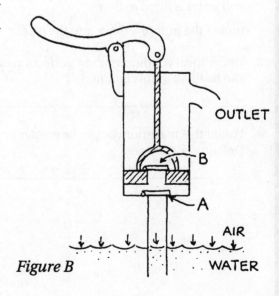

Figure B

CONCEPTUAL PHYSICS

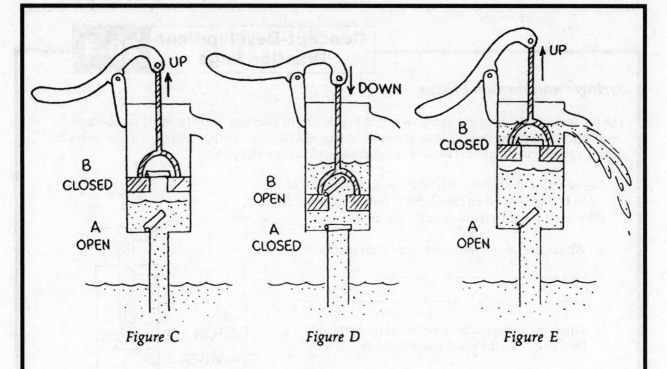

Figure C   *Figure D*   *Figure E*

When the piston is raised (Figure C), air pressure is reduced in the pipe that extends into the water. This allows water from below to be pushed up into the pipe by

(atmospheric pressure)   (a vacuum).

Valve A opens as water enters the chamber. When the piston is pushed down (Figure D), valve A closes and valve B

(closes also)   (opens).

This lets water enter the chamber above the piston. When the piston is lifted again (Figure E), Valve B

(closes)   (opens)

and water is lifted to flow

(out of the pump)   (back into the pipe).

3. Under ideal conditions and a perfect vacuum, what is the maximum height that water at sea level can be lifted in this manner?

_____

4. Would this maximum height be greater or less for a lift pump high in the mountains? Defend your answer.

_____

CONCEPTUAL PHYSICS

Concept-Development Practice Page | 20-2

Gases

1. A principle difference between a liquid and a gas is that when a liquid is under pressure, its volume

    (increases)   (decreases)   (doesn't change noticeably)

    and its density

    (increases)   (decreases)   (doesn't change noticeably).

    When a gas is under pressure, its volume

    (increases)   (decreases)   (doesn't change noticeably)

    and its density

    (increases)   (decreases)   (doesn't change noticeably).

2. The sketch shows the launching of a weather balloon at sea level. Make a sketch of the same weather balloon when it is high in the atmosphere. In words, what is different about its size and why?

    _____

    _____

    _____

    _____

HIGH-ALTITUDE SIZE

GROUND-LEVEL SIZE

3. A hydrogen-filled balloon that weighs 10 N must displace _____N of air in order to float in air.

    If it displaces less than _____N, it will be buoyed up with less than _____N and sink.

    If it displaces more than _____N of air, it will move upward.

4. Why is the cartoon more humorous to physics types than to non-physics types? What physics has occurred?

    _____

    _____

    _____

    _____

RATS TO YOU TOO, DANIEL BERNOULLI!

CONCEPTUAL PHYSICS

Concept-Development Practice Page **21-1**

Temperature and Heat

1. Complete the table.

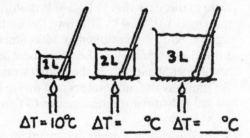

TEMPERATURE OF MELTING ICE	°C	32 °F	K
TEMPERATURE OF BOILING WATER	°C	212°F	K

2. Suppose you apply a flame and heat one liter of water, raising its temperature 10°C. If you transfer the same heat energy to two liters, how much will the temperature rise? For three liters? Record your answers on the blanks in the drawing at the right.

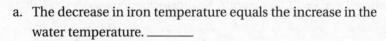

ΔT = 10°C   ΔT = ___°C   ΔT = ___°C

3. A thermometer is in a container half-filled with 20°C water.

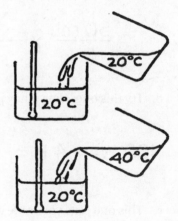

   a. When an equal volume of 20°C water is added, the temperature of the mixture is

      (10°C)   (20°C)   (40°C).

   b. When instead an equal volume of 40°C water is added, the temperature of the mixture will be

      (20°C)   (30°C)   (40°C).

   c. When instead a small amount of 40°C water is added, the temperature of the mixture will be

      (20°C)   (between 20°C and 30°C)   (30°C)   (more than 30°C).

4. A red-hot piece of iron is put into a bucket of cool water. *Mark the following statements true (T) or false (F).* (Ignore heat transfer to the bucket.)

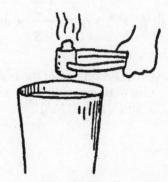

   a. The decrease in iron temperature equals the increase in the water temperature. _____

   b. The quantity of heat lost by the iron equals the quantity of heat gained by the water. _____

   c. The iron and water both will reach the same temperature. _____

   d. The final temperature of the iron and water is halfway between the initial temperatures of each. _____

CAN COMMON ICE BE COLDER THAN 0°C?

CONCEPTUAL PHYSICS

5. The Do the Math! example on page 412 of your textbook shows the technique of unit conversion, called *dimensional analysis,* which indicates whether to multiply or divide when converting one quantity to another. The example converts Calories per day to watts. The *conversion factors* used in the example are (1 day)/(24 hours), (1 hour)/(3600 seconds), and (4184 joules)/(1 Calorie). The Calorie here is the "big" Calorie, commonly used in rating foods. Note carefully how the units cancel just as numbers do when multiplying fractions.

We will use this technique to solve the following: How many joules of energy are transferred per day at the rate of 1 watt? We know that 1 W is equal to 1 J/s. So

$$\frac{1\text{ J}}{1\text{ s}} \times \frac{3600\text{ s}}{1\text{ h}} \times \frac{24\text{ h}}{1\text{ d}} = \underline{\hspace{2cm}} \text{ J/d}$$

Note in this case that (1 J)/(1 s) is multiplied by (3600 s)/(1 h) rather than by (1 h)/(3600 s). This way, the units s cancel. The same is true for units h. So 1 J is multiplied by 3600, since there are 3600 seconds in 1 hour, and again by 24, because there are 24 hours in 1 day. These numbers appear only in the numerators, so they are simply multiplied. We multiply the numerators and divide by the denominators. In this case we see only the numerical values of 1 appear in the demoninators.

a. By *dimensional analysis* convert 50 calories per hour *(small* calories) to joules per day.

$$\frac{50\text{ cal}}{1\text{ h}} \times \frac{\text{h}}{\text{d}} \times \frac{\text{J}}{\text{cal}} = \underline{\hspace{1.5cm}}$$

b. Try this one: How many joules will a 100-watt bulb give off in 4 hours?

$$100\text{ W} \times 4\text{ h} = \underline{\hspace{1cm}}\frac{\text{J}}{\text{s}} \times 4\text{ h} \times \underline{\hspace{1cm}}\frac{\text{s}}{\text{h}} = \underline{\hspace{3cm}}\text{ J}$$

c. This one puts you more on your own: Find the number of joules given off by a 4-W bulb in a night light that burns continously for one month (1 mo).

$$4\text{ W} \times 1\text{ mo} = \frac{4\text{ J}}{1\text{ s}} \times 1\text{ mo} \times \underline{\hspace{4cm}} = \underline{\hspace{2cm}}\text{ J}$$

6. On a certain planet the unit of heat energy is called the OOH, where 1 OOH = 3 calories, and the unit of time is called the AAH, where 1 AAH = 12.56 seconds. By *dimensional analysis* show that 1 watt = 1 OOH/AAH.

Thermal Expansion

1.　Long steel bridges often have one end fixed while the other end rests on rockers, as shown. Each sketch shows the bridge at a different season of the year. Mark the sketches winter (W) or summer (S). Briefly defend your answer.

_____

_____

_____

_____

_____

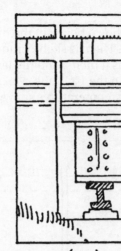

( )　　　　( )

2.　The weight hangs above the floor from the copper wire. When a candle is moved along the wire and heats it, what happens to the height of the weight above the floor? Why?

_____

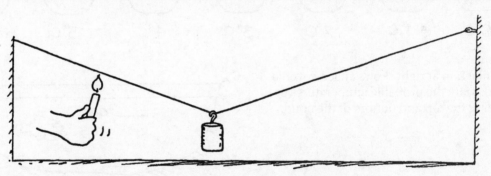

3.　A steel television broadcasting tower is taller in the daytime than it is in the cooler nighttime. This is because steel expands (or contracts) about 1 part in 100,000 for each degree Celsius change. By this we mean that a piece of steel 100,000 units long will be 100,001 units long when its temperature increases by 1°C. What is the change in height for a 500-m steel tower when its temperature changes 20°C from day to night?

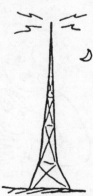

_____ cm

4. A common saying is "water seeks its own level," and usually it does. Here we see a container of water that is cooled on the left and warmed on the right. Consider the effect of temperature on density. Compared to the water level in the right tube, the water level in the left tube is

(slightly higher)   (slightly lower)   (the same).

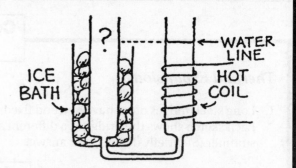

5. The levels of water at 0°C and 1°C are shown below in the first two flasks. At these temperatures there is microscopic slush in the water. There is slightly more slush at 0°C than at 1°C. As the water is heated, some of the slush collapses as it melts, and the level of the water falls in the tube. That's why the level of water is slightly lower in the 1°C-tube. Make rough estimates and sketch in the appropriate levels of water at the other temperatures shown. What is important about the level when the water reaches 4°C?

_____

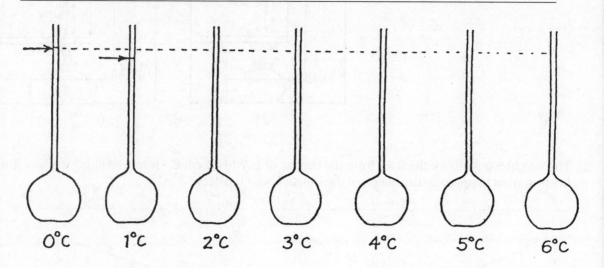

6. The diagram at right shows an ice-covered pond. Mark the probable temperatures of water at the top and bottom of the pond.

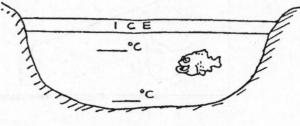

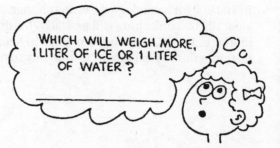

CONCEPTUAL PHYSICS

**Concept-Development
Practice Page** | **22-1**

Transmission of Heat

1. The tips of both brass rods are held in the gas flame. *Mark the following true (T) or false (F).*

   a. Heat is conducted only along Rod A. _____

   b. Heat is conducted only along Rod B. _____

   c. Heat is conducted equally along both Rod A and Rod B. _____

   d. The idea that "heat rises" applies to heat transfer by *convection,* not by *conduction.* _____

2.  Why does a bird fluff its feathers to keep warm on a cold day?

   _____

3. Why does a down-filled sleeping bag keep you warm on a cold night? Why is it useless if the down is wet?

   _____

   _____

4. What does *convection* have to do with the holes in the shade of the desk lamp?

   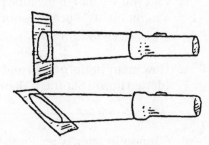

   _____

5. The warmth of equatorial regions and coldness of polar regions on Earth can be understood by considering light from a flashlight striking a surface. If it strikes perpendicularly, light energy is more concentrated as it covers a smaller area; if it strikes at an angle, the energy spreads over a larger area. So the energy per unit area is less.

   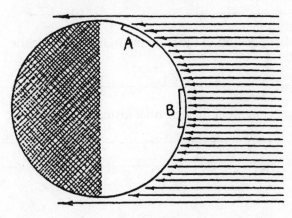

   The arrows represent rays of light from the distant sun incident upon Earth. Two areas of equal size are shown, Area A near the north pole and Area B near the equator. Count the rays that reach each area, and explain why B is warmer than A.

   _____

   _____

CONCEPTUAL PHYSICS

6. Earth's seasons result from the 23.5-degree tilt of Earth's daily spin axis as it orbits the sun. When Earth is at the point shown on the right in the sketch below (not to scale), the Northern Hemisphere tilts toward the sun, and sunlight striking it is strong (more rays per area). Sunlight striking the Southern Hemisphere is weak (fewer rays per area). Days in the north are warmer, and daylight is longer. You can see this by imagining Earth making its complete daily 24-hour spin.

Do two things on the sketch: (1) Shade the part of Earth in nighttime darkness for all positions, as is already done in the left position. (2) Label each position with the proper month — March, June, September, or December.

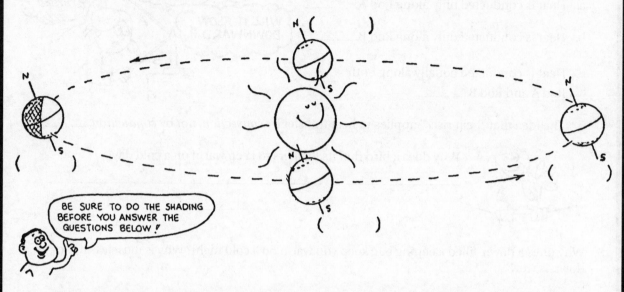

BE SURE TO DO THE SHADING BEFORE YOU ANSWER THE QUESTIONS BELOW!

a. When Earth is in any of the four positions shown, during one 24-hour spin a location at the equator receives sunlight half the time and is in darkness the other half the time.
This means that regions at the equator always get about _____ hours of sunlight and _____ hours of darkness.

b. Can you see that in the June position regions farther north have longer daylight hours and shorter nights? Locations north of the Arctic Circle (dotted line in Northern Hemisphere) always face toward the sun as Earth spins, so they get daylight _____ hours a day.

c. How many hours of light and darkness are there in June at regions south of the Antarctic Circle (dotted line in Southern Hemisphere)?

_____

d. Six months later, when Earth is at the December position, is the situation in the Antarctic the same or is it the reverse?

_____

e. Why do South America and Australia enjoy warm weather in December instead of June?

_____

_____

CONCEPTUAL PHYSICS

Change of Phase

All matter can exist in the solid, liquid, or gaseous phases. The solid phase exists at relatively low temperatures, the liquid phase at higher temperatures, and the gaseous phase at still higher temperatures. Water is the most common example, not only because of its abundance but also because the temperatures for all three phases are common. Study Section 23.8 in your textbook and then answer the following:

1. How many calories are needed to change 1 gram of 0°C ice to water?

   _____

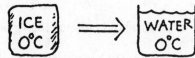

2. How many calories are needed to change the temperature of 1 gram of water by 1°C?

   _____

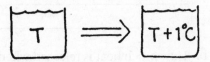

3. How many calories are needed to melt 1 gram of 0°C ice and turn it to water at a room temperature of 23°C?

   _____

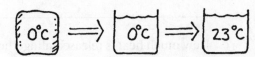

4. A 50-gram sample of ice at 0°C is placed in a glass beaker that contains 200 g of water at 20°C.

   a. How much heat is needed to melt the ice? _____

   b. By how much would the temperature of the water change if it gave up this much heat to the ice? _____

   c. What will be the final temperature of the mixture? (Disregard any heat absorbed by the glass or given off by the surrounding air.) _____

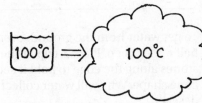

5. How many calories are needed to change 1 gram of 100°C boiling water to 100°C steam?

   _____

6. Fill in the number of calories at each step below for changing the state of 1 gram of 0°C ice to 100°C steam.

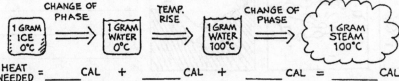

CONCEPTUAL PHYSICS

7. One gram of steam at 100°C condenses, and the water cools to 22°C.

   a. How much heat is released when the steam condenses? _____

   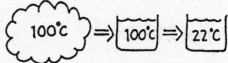

   b. How much heat is released when the water cools from 100°C to 22°C?

   _____

   c. How much heat is released altogether? _____

8. In a household radiator 1000 g of steam at 100°C condenses, and the water cools to 90°C.

   a. How much heat is released when the steam condenses?

   _____

   _____

   b. How much heat is released when the water cools from 100°C to 90°C?

   _____

   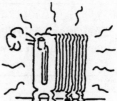

   c. How much heat is released altogether?

   _____

9. Why is it difficult to make tea on the top of a high mountain?

   _____

10. How many calories are given up by 1 gram of 100°C steam that condenses to 100°C water?

   _____

11. How many calories are given up by 1 gram of 100°C steam that condenses and drops in temperature to 22°C water?

   _____

12. How many calories are given to a household radiator when 1000 grams of 100°C steam condenses, and drops in temperature to 90°C water?

   _____

13. To get water from the ground, even in the hot desert, dig a hole about a half meter wide and a half meter deep. Place a cup at the bottom. Spread a sheet of plastic wrap over the hole and place stones along the edge to hold it secure. Weight the center of the plastic with a stone so it forms a cone shape. Why will water collect in the cup? (Physics can save your life if you're ever stranded in a desert!)

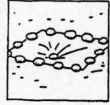

   _____

   _____

   _____

   _____

CONCEPTUAL PHYSICS

Concept-Development Practice Page 23-2

Evaporation

1. Why does it feel colder when you swim at a pool on a windy day?

   _____

2. Why does your skin feel cold when a little rubbing alcohol is applied to it?

   _____

3. Briefly explain from a molecular point of view why evaporation is a cooling process.

   _____

   _____

4. When hot water rapidly evaporates, the result can be dramatic. Consider 4 g of boiling water spread over a large surface so that 1 g rapidly evaporates. Suppose further that the surface and surroundings are very cold so that all 540 calories for evaporation come from the remaining 3 g of water.

   a. How many calories are taken from each gram of water?

   _____

   b. How many calories are released when 1 g of 100°C water cools to 0°C?

   _____

   c. How many calories are released when 1 g of 0°C water changes to 0°C ice?

   _____

   d. What happens in this case to the remaining 3 g of boiling water when 1 g rapidly evaporates?

   _____

   _____

CONCEPTUAL PHYSICS

Our Earth's Hot Interior

A major puzzle faced scientists in the nineteenth century. Volcanoes showed that Earth is molten beneath its crust. Penetration into the crust by bore holes and mines showed that Earth's temperature increases with depth. Scientists found that heat flows from the interior to the surface. They assumed that the source of Earth's internal heat was primordial, the afterglow of its fiery birth. Measurements of cooling rates indicated a relatively young Earth—some 25 to 30 millions years in age. But geological evidence indicated an older Earth. This puzzle wasn't solved until the discovery of radioactivity. Then it was learned that the interior is kept hot by the energy of radioactive decay. We now know the age of Earth is some 4.5 billions years—a much older Earth.

All rock contains trace amounts of radioactive minerals. Those in common granite release energy at the rate 0.03 joule/kilogram·year. Granite at Earth's surface transfers this energy to the surroundings as fast as it is generated, so we don't find granite warm to the touch. But what if a sample of granite were thermally insulated? That is, suppose the increase of internal energy due to radioactivity were contained. Then it would get hotter. How much? Let's figure it out, using 790 joule/kilogram·kelvin as the specific heat of granite.

Calculations to make:

1. How many joules are required to increase the temperature of 1 kg of granite by 1000 K?

   _____

2. How many years would it take radioactive decay in a kilogram of granite to produce this many joules?

   _____

Questions to answer:

3. How many years would it take a thermally insulated 1-kg chunk of granite to undergo a 1000 K increase in temperature?

   _____

4. How many years would it take a thermally insulated one-million-kilogram chunk of granite to undergo a 1000 K increase in temperature?

   _____

5. Why are your answers to the above the same (or different)?

   _____

   _____

   _____

An electric toaster stays hot while electric energy is supplied, and doesn't cool until switched off. Similarly, do you think the energy source now keeping Earth hot will one day suddenly switch off like a disconnected toaster — or gradually decrease over a long time?

Circle one:

6. The energy produced by Earth radioactivity ultimately becomes terrestrial radiation. (True) (False)

CONCEPTUAL PHYSICS

Class _____ Date _____

Thermodynamics

A mass of air is contained so that the volume can change but the pressure
remains constant. Table I shows air volumes at various temperatures when
the air is heated slowly.

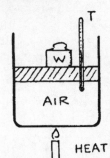

1. Plot the data in Table I on the graph, and connect the points.

Table I

TEMP. (°C)	VOLUME (mL)
0	50
25	55
50	60
75	65
100	70

VOLUME (mL)

70
60
50
40
30
20
10

-200   -100   0   50   100

TEMPERATURE (°C)

2. The graph shows how the volume of air varies with temperature at constant pressure. The
straightness of the line means that the air expands uniformly with temperature. From your graph,
you can predict what will happen to the volume of air when it is cooled.

Extrapolate (extend) the straight line of your graph to find the temperature at which the volume of
the air would become zero. Mark this point on your graph. Estimate this
temperature: _____

3. Although air would liquify before cooling to this temperature, the procedure suggests that there
is a lower limit to how cold something can be. This is the absolute zero of temperature. Careful
experiments show that absolute zero is _____°C.

4. Scientists measure temperature in *kelvins* instead of degrees Celsius, where the absolute zero of
temperature is 0 kelvins. If you relabeled the temperature axis on the graph in Question 1 so that it
shows temperature in kelvins, would your graph look like the one below? _____

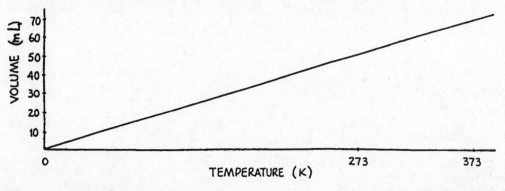

CONCEPTUAL PHYSICS

Concept-Development Practice Page | **25-1**

Vibrations and Waves

1. A sine curve that represents a transverse wave is drawn below. With a ruler, measure the wavelength and amplitude of the wave.

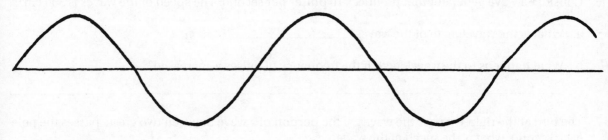

   a. Wavelength = _____

   b. Amplitude = _____

2. A kid on a playground swing makes a complete to-and-fro swing each 2 seconds. The frequency of swing is

     (0.5 hertz) (1 hertz) (2 hertz)

  and the period is

     (0.5 second) (1 second) (2 seconds).

3. *Complete the statements.*

THE PERIOD OF A 440-HERTZ SOUND WAVE IS _____ SECOND.

A MARINE WEATHER STATION REPORTS WAVES ALONG THE SHORE THAT ARE 8 SECONDS APART. THE FREQUENCY OF THE WAVES IS THEREFORE _____ HERTZ.

4. The annoying sound from a mosquito is produced when it beats its wings at the average rate of 600 wingbeats per second.

   a. What is the frequency of the soundwaves?

   _____

   b. What is the wavelength? (Assume the speed of sound is 340 m/s.)

   _____

CONCEPTUAL PHYSICS

5. A pitching machine goes haywire and pitches at 10 rounds per second. The speed of the balls is an incredible 300 m/s.

   a. What is the distance in the air between the flying balls? _____

   b. What happens to the distance between the balls if the rate of pitching is increased?

   _____

6. Consider a wave generator that produces 10 pulses per second. The speed of the waves is 300 cm/s.

   a. What is the wavelength of the waves? _____

   b. What happens to the wavelength if the frequency of pulses is increased?

   _____

7. The bird at the right watches the waves. If the portion of a wave between two crests passes the pole each second, what is the speed of the wave?

   _____

   What is its period?

   _____

   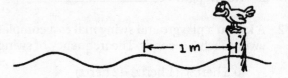

8. If the distance between crests in the above question was 1.5 meters, and two crests pass the pole each second, what would be the speed of the wave?

   _____

   What would be its period?

   _____

9. When an automobile moves toward a listener, the sound of its horn seems relatively

   (low pitched) (normal)

   (high pitched)

   and when moving away from the listener, its horn seems

   (low pitched) (normal)

   (high pitched).

10. The changed pitch of the Doppler effect is due to changes in (wave speed) (wave frequency).

Shock Waves

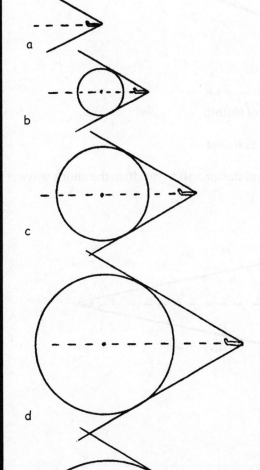

The cone-shaped shock wave produced by a super-sonic aircraft is actually the result of overlapping spherical waves of sound, as shown in Figure 25.22 in your textbook. Sketches (a), (b), (c), (d), and (e) at the left show the "animated" growth of only one of the many spherical sound waves (shown as an expanding circle in the two-dimensional sketch). The circle originates when the aircraft is in the position shown in (a). Sketch (b) shows both the growth of the circle and position of the aircraft at a later time. Still later times are shown in (c), (d), and (e). Note that the circle grows and the aircraft moves farther to the right. Note also that the aircraft is moving farther than the sound wave. This is because the aircraft is moving faster than sound.

Careful examination will reveal how fast the aircraft is moving compared to the speed of sound. Sketch (e) shows that in the same time the sound travels from O to A, the aircraft has traveled from O to B — twice as far. You can check this with a ruler.

Circle the correct answers.

1. Inspect sketches (b) and (d). Has the aircraft traveled twice as far as sound in the same time in these postions also?

   (Yes) (No)

2. For greater speeds, the angle of the shock wave would be

   (wider) (the same) (narrower).

CONCEPTUAL PHYSICS

3. Use a ruler to estimate the speeds of the aircraft that produce the shock waves in the two sketches below.

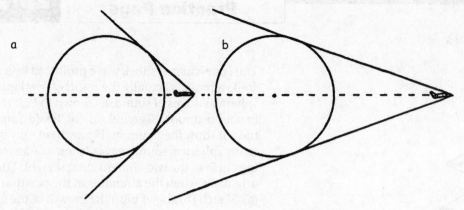

Aircraft (a) is traveling about _____ times the speed of sound.

Aircraft (b) is traveling about _____ times the speed of sound.

4. Draw your own circle (anywhere) and estimate the speed of the aircraft to produce the shock wave shown below.

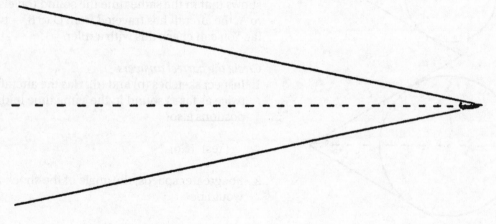

The speed is about _____ times the speed of sound.

5. In the space below, draw the shock wave made by a supersonic missile that travels at four times the speed of sound.

**Concept-Development
Practice Page** **25-3**

Wave Superposition

A pair of pulses travel toward each other at equal speeds. The composite waveforms as they pass through each other and interfere are shown at 1-second intervals. In the left column, note how the pulses interfere to produce the composite waveform (solid line). Make a similar construction for the two wave pulses in the right column. Like the pulses in the first column, they each travel at 1 space per second.

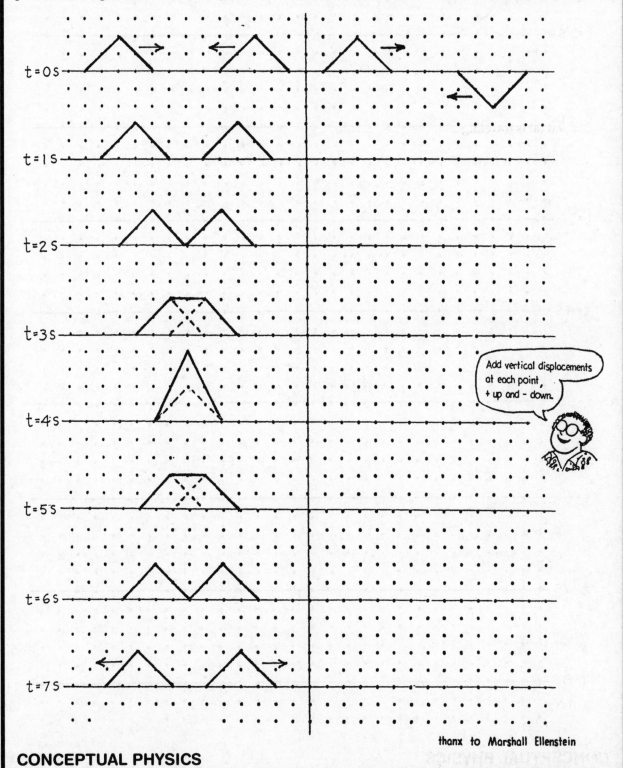

Add vertical displacements at each point, + up and – down.

thanx to Marshall Ellenstein

CONCEPTUAL PHYSICS

Construct the composite waveforms at 1-second intervals for the two waves traveling toward each other at equal speed.

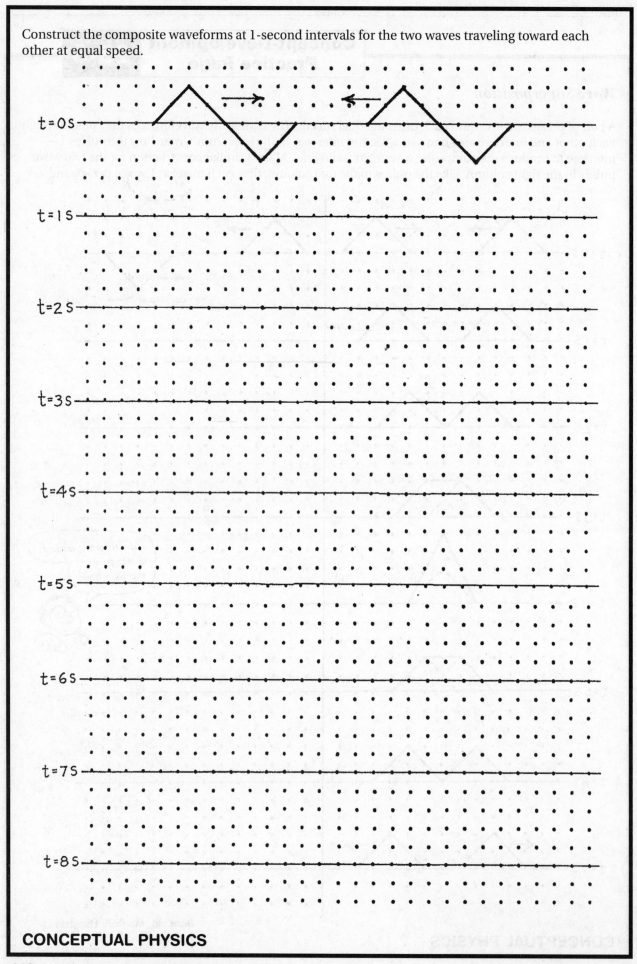

Sound

1. Two major classes of waves are *longitudinal* and *transverse*. Sound waves are
   (longitudinal) (transverse).

2. The frequency of a sound signal refers to how frequently the
   vibrations occur. A high-frequency sound is heard at a high
   (pitch) (wavelength) (speed).

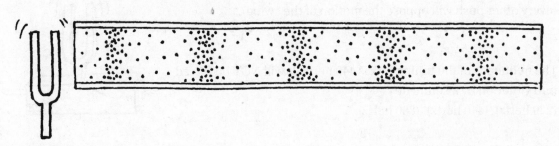

3. The sketch below shows a snapshot of the compressions and rarefactions of the air in a tube as the
   sound moves toward the right. The dots represent molecules. With a ruler, the wavelength of the
   sound wave is measured to be ___2.5___ cm.

4. Compared to the wavelengths of high-pitched sounds, the wavelengths of low-pitched sounds are
   (long) (short).

5. Suppose you set your watch by the sound of the noon whistle from a factory 3 km away.

   a. Compared to the correct time, your watch will be
      (behind) (ahead).

   b. It will differ from the correct time by
      (3 seconds) (6 seconds) (9 seconds).

LET'S SEE, FROM $v = \dfrac{d}{t}$

$t = \dfrac{d}{v} = \dfrac{3000 \text{ m}}{340 \text{ m/s}} = \ldots$

PHYSICS
PHYSICS

CONCEPTUAL PHYSICS

6. Sound waves travel fastest in
   (solids) (liquids) (gases)
   (...same speed in each).

7. If the child's natural frequency of swinging is once each
   4 seconds, for maximum amplitude the man should
   push at a rate of once each
   (2 seconds) (4 seconds) (8 seconds).

8. If the man in Question 7 pushes in the same direction
   twice as often, his pushes
   (will) (will not)
   be effective because
   (the swing will be pushed twice as often in the right direction)
   (every other push will oppose the motion of the swing).

9. The frequency of the tuning fork is 440 hertz. It will NOT be forced
   into vibration by a sound of
   (220 hertz) (440 hertz) (880 hertz).

10. Beats are the result of the alternate cancellation and reinforcement of two sound waves of
    (the same frequency) (slightly different frequencies).

11. Two notes with frequencies of 66 and
    70 Hz are sounded together. The resulting
    beat frequency is
    (4 hertz) (68 hertz) (136 hertz).

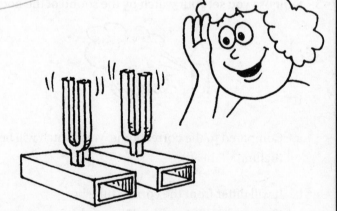

12. The accepted value for the speed of sound in air is 332 m/s at 0°C. The speed of sound in air
    increases 0.6 m/s for each Celsius degree above zero. Compute the speed of sound at the
    temperature of the room you are now in.

    Temp = 23 °C   332 + 14 = 346 m/s

    23 · 0 · 6 = 13.8

Concept-Development Practice Page 27-1

Light

1. The Danish astronomer Olaus Roemer made careful measurements of the period of a moon about the planet Jupiter. How this data enabled a calculation of the speed of light is described in your textbook on pages 534 and 535.

   a. What is the diameter, in kilometers, of Earth's orbit around the sun?

   _____

   b. How much time is required for light to travel across the diameter of the orbit?

   _____

   c. How do these two quantities determine the speed of light?

   _____

2. Study Figure 27.4 on page 536 in your textbook and answer the following:

   a. Which have longer *wavelengths*, radio waves or light waves?

   _____

   b. Which have longer *wavelengths*, light waves or gamma rays?

   _____

   c. Which have higher *frequencies*, ultraviolet or infrared waves?

   _____

   d. Which have higher *frequencies*, ultraviolet waves or gamma rays?

   _____

3. Carefully study Section 27.4 in your textbook and answer the following:

   a. Exactly what do vibrating electrons emit?

   _____

   b. When ultraviolet light shines on glass, what does it do to electrons in the glass structure?

   _____

   c. When energetic electrons in the glass structure vibrate against neighboring atoms, what happens to the energy of vibration?

   _____

   d. What happens to the energy of a vibrating electron that does not collide with neighboring atoms?

   _____

CONCEPTUAL PHYSICS

e. Which range of light frequencies, visible or ultraviolet, is absorbed in glass?

_____

f. Which range of light frequencies, visible or ultraviolet, is transmitted through glass?

_____

g. How is the speed of light in glass affected by the succession of time delays that accompany the absorption and re-emission of light from atom to atom in the glass?

_____

h. How does the speed of light compare in water, glass, and diamond?

_____

4. The sun normally shines on both Earth and the moon. Both cast shadows. Sometimes the moon's shadow falls on Earth and, at other times, Earth's shadow falls on the moon.

a. The sketch shows the sun and Earth. Draw the moon at a position for a solar eclipse.

b. This sketch also shows the sun and Earth. Draw the moon at a position for a lunar eclipse.

5. The diagram shows the limits of light rays when a large lamp makes a shadow of a small object on a screen. Shade the umbra darker than the penumbra. In what part of the shadow could an ant see part of the lamp?

_____

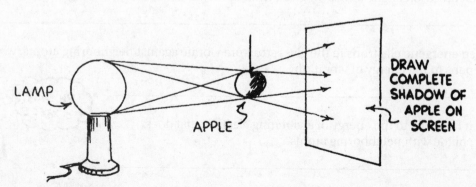

LAMP   APPLE   DRAW COMPLETE SHADOW OF APPLE ON SCREEN

CONCEPTUAL PHYSICS

Concept-Development Practice Page 27-2

Polarization

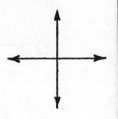

The amplitude of a light wave has magnitude and direction and can be represented by a vector. Polarized light vibrates in a single direction and is represented by a single vector. To the left, the single vector represents vertically polarized light. The vibrations of non-polarized light are equal in all directions. There are as many vertical components as horizontal components. The pair of perpendicular vectors to the right represents non-polarized light.

1. In the sketch below, non-polarized light from a flashlight strikes a pair of polarizing filters.

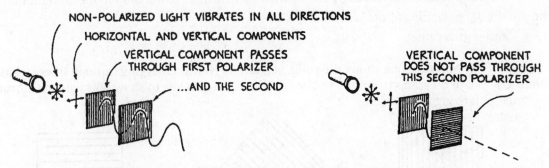

NON-POLARIZED LIGHT VIBRATES IN ALL DIRECTIONS

HORIZONTAL AND VERTICAL COMPONENTS

VERTICAL COMPONENT PASSES THROUGH FIRST POLARIZER

...AND THE SECOND

VERTICAL COMPONENT DOES NOT PASS THROUGH THIS SECOND POLARIZER

a. Light is transmitted by a pair of polarizing filters when their axes are

(aligned) (crossed at right angles)

and light is blocked when their axes are

(aligned) (crossed at right angles).

b. Transmitted light is polarized in a direction

(the same as) (different than) the polarization axis of the filter.

2. Consider the transmission of light through a pair of polarizing filters with polarization axes at 45° to each other. Although in practice the polarizing filters are one atop the other, we show them spread out side by side below. From left to right: (a) Non-polarized light is represented by its horizontal and vertical components. (b) These components strike filter A. (c) The vertical component is transmitted, and (d) falls upon filter B. This vertical component is not aligned with the polarization axis of filter B, but it has a component that is — component **t**; (e) which is transmitted.

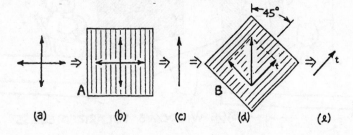

(a)   (b)   (c)   (d)   (e)

a. The amount of light that gets through Filter B, compared to the amount that gets through Filter A is (more) (less) (the same).

b. The component perpendicular to **t** that falls on Filter B is (also transmitted) (absorbed).

CONCEPTUAL PHYSICS

3. Below are a pair of polarizing filters with polarization axes at 30° to each other. Carefully draw vectors and appropriate components (as in Question 2) to show the vector that emerges at (e).

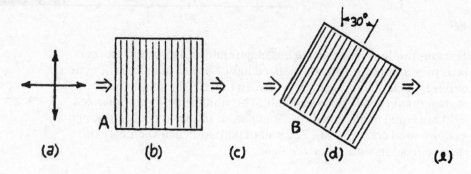

(a) (b) (c) (d) (e)

The amount of light that gets through the polarizing filters at 30° compared to the amount that gets though the 45° polarizing filters is

(less) (more) (the same).

4. Figure 27.17 in your textbook shows the smile of Ludmila Hewitt emerging through three polarizing filters. Use vector diagrams to complete steps (b) through (g) below to show how light gets through the three-polarizing filter system.

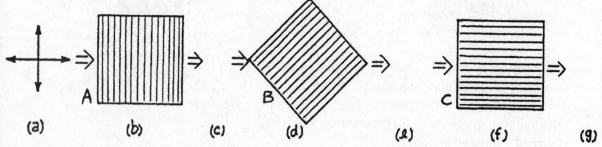

(a) (b) (c) (d) (e) (f) (g)

5. A novel use of polarization is shown below. How do the polarized side windows in these next-to-each-other houses provide privacy for the occupants? (Who can see what?)

SIDE WINDOWS POLARIZED GLASS

CONCEPTUAL PHYSICS

Concept-Development Practice Page | 28-1

Color

1. The sketch shows the shadow of your hand held in front of a white screen in a darkened room. The light source is red, so the screen looks red and the shadow looks black. Color the sketch with colored markers, or label the colors with pen or pencil.

2. A green lamp is turned on and makes a second shadow. The formerly black shadow cast by the red light is no longer black, but is illuminated with green light. So it is green. Color or mark it green. The shadow cast by the green lamp is not black because it is illuminated with the red light. Color or mark its color. The background receives a mixture of red and green light. Figure out what color the background will appear; then color or label it.

3. A blue lamp is turned on and three shadows of your hand appear. Color or label the appropriate colors of the shadows and the background.

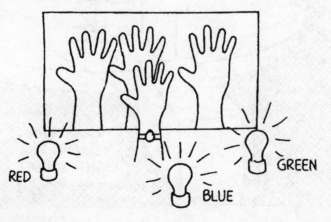

CONCEPTUAL PHYSICS

4. If you have colored markers, have a go at these.

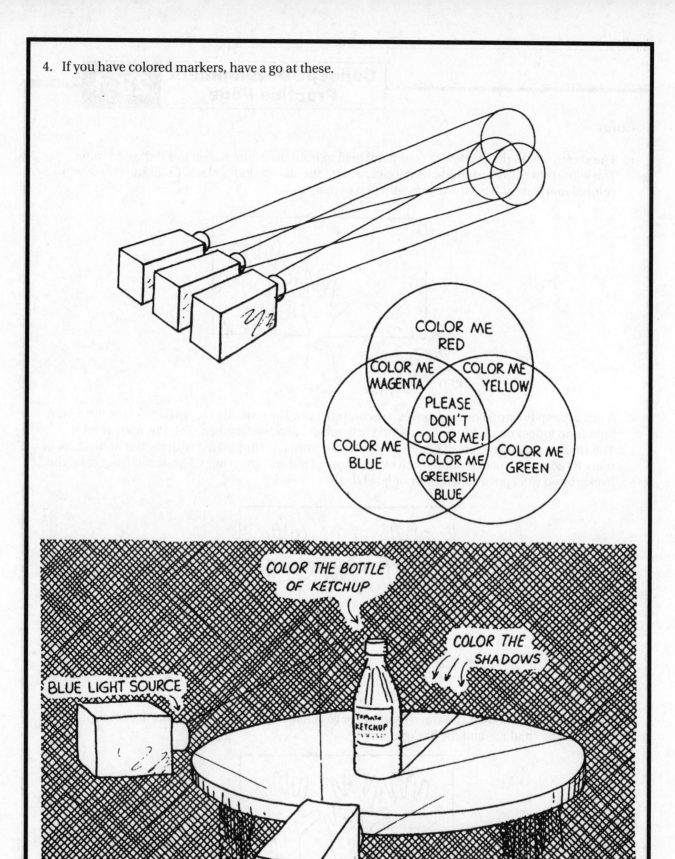

CONCEPTUAL PHYSICS

Reflection

1. Light from a flashlight shines on a mirror and illuminates one of the cards. Draw the reflected beam to indicate the illuminated card.

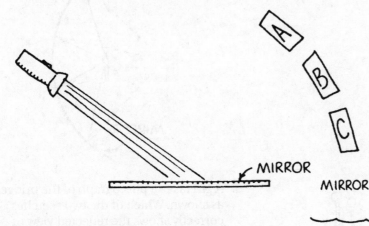

2. A periscope has a pair of mirrors in it. Draw the light path from the object O to the eye of the observer.

3. The ray diagram below shows the extension of one of the reflected rays from the plane mirror. Complete the diagram by (1) carefully drawing the three other reflected rays, and (2) extending them behind the mirror to locate the image of the flame. (Assume the candle and image are viewed by an observer on the left.)

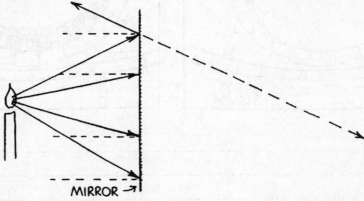

CONCEPTUAL PHYSICS

4. The ray diagram below shows the reflection of one of the rays that strikes the parabolic mirror. Notice that the law of reflection is obeyed, and the angle of incidence (from the normal, the dashed line) equals the angle of reflection (from the normal). Complete the diagram by drawing the reflected rays of the other three rays that are shown. (Do you see why parabolic mirrors are used in automobile headlights?)

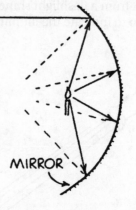

MIRROR

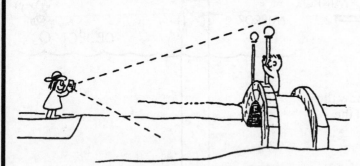

5. A girl takes a photograph of the bridge as shown. Which of the two sketches correctly shows the reflected view of the bridge? Defend your answer.

CONCEPTUAL PHYSICS

Reflection

  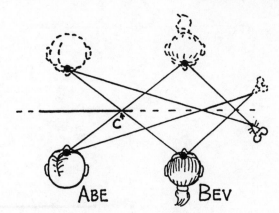

← MIRROR

ABE   BEV   ABE   BEV

Abe and Bev both look in a plane mirror directly in front of Abe (left, top view). Abe can see himself while Bev cannot see herself—but can Abe see Bev, and can Bev see Abe? To find the answer we construct their artificial locations "through" the mirror, the same distance behind as Abe and Bev are in front (right, top view). If straight-line connections intersect the mirror, as at point C, then each sees the other. The mouse, for example, cannot see or be seen by Abe and Bev.

Here we have eight students in front of a small plane mirror. Their positions are shown in the diagram below. Make appropriate straight-line constructions to answer the following:

←MIRROR

ABE   BEV   CIS   DON   EVA   FLO   GUY   HAN

Who can Abe see? _____	Who can Abe not see? _____
Who can Bev see? _____	Who can Bev not see? _____
Who can Cis see? _____	Who can Cis not see? _____
Who can Don see? _____	Who can Don not see? _____
Who can Eva see? _____	Who can Eva not see? _____
Who can Flo see? _____	Who can Flo not see? _____
Who can Guy see? _____	Who can Guy not see? _____
Who can Han see? _____	Who can Han not see? _____

thanx to Marshall Ellenstein

CONCEPTUAL PHYSICS

Six of our group are now arranged differently in front of the same mirror. Their positions are shown below. Make appropriate constructions for this more interesting arrangement, and answer the questions below.

ABE

EVA

BEV

FLO

CIS

DON

Who can Abe see? _____ Who can Abe not see? _____

Who can Bev see? _____ Who can Bev not see? _____

Who can Cis see? _____ Who can Cis not see? _____

Who can Don see? _____ Who can Don not see? _____

Who can Eva see? _____ Who can Eva not see? _____

Who can Flo see? _____ Who can Flo not see? _____

Harry Hotshot views himself in a full-length mirror (right). Construct straight lines from Harry's eyes to the image of his feet and to the top of his head. Mark the mirror to indicate the minimum area Harry uses to see a full view of himself.

Does this region of the mirror depend on Harry's distance from the mirror?

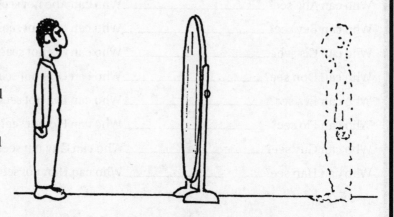

CONCEPTUAL PHYSICS

Refraction

1. A pair of toy cart wheels that can spin independently are rolled obliquely from a smooth surface onto two plots of grass — a rectangular plot as shown at the left, and a triangular plot as shown at the right. The ground is on a slight incline so that after slowing down in the grass, the wheels speed up again when emerging on the smooth surface. Finish each sketch and show some positions of the wheels inside the plots and on the other side. Clearly indicate their paths and directions of travel.

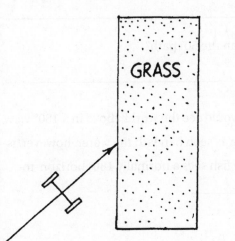 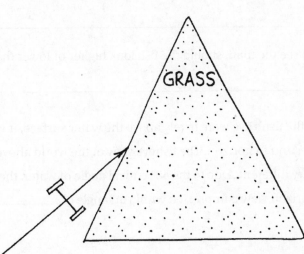

2. Red, green, and blue rays of light are incident upon a glass prism as shown. The average speed of red light in the glass is less than in air, so the red ray is refracted. When it emerges into the air it regains its original speed and travels in the direction shown. Green light takes longer to get through the glass. Because of its slower speed it is refracted as shown. Blue light travels even slower in glass. Complete the diagram by estimating the path of the blue ray.

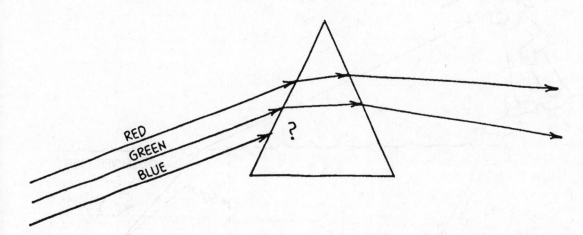

3. The sketch shows that due to refraction, the man sees the fish closer to the water surface than it actually is.

   a. Draw a ray beginning at the fish's eye to show the line of sight of the fish when it looks upward at 50° to the normal at the water surface. Draw the direction of the ray after it meets the surface of the water and continues in the air.

   b. At the 50° angle, does the fish see the man, or does it see the reflected view of the starfish at the bottom of the pond? Explain.

   _____

   _____

   c. To see the man, should the fish look higher or lower than the 50° path?

   _____

   d. If the fish's eye were barely above the water surface, it would see the world above in a 180° view, horizon to horizon. The fisheye view of the world above as seen beneath the water, however, is very different. Due to the 48° critical angle of water, the fish sees a normally 180° horizon-to-horizon view compressed within an angle of _____.

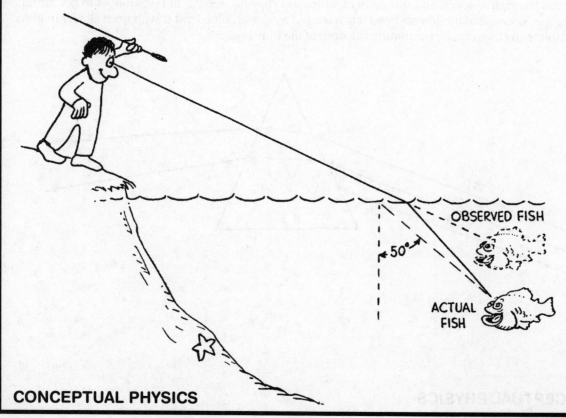

CONCEPTUAL PHYSICS

Concept-Development Practice Page **29-4**

Refraction

1. The sketch to the right shows a light ray moving from air into water at 45° to the normal. Which of the three rays indicated with capital letters is most likely the light ray that continues inside the water?

_____

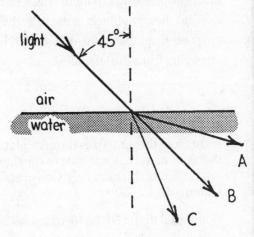

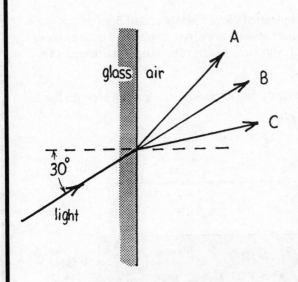

2. The sketch on the left shows a light ray moving from glass into air at 30° to the normal. Which of the three is most likely the light ray that continues in the air?

_____

3. To the right, a light ray is shown moving from air into a glass block at 40° to the normal. Which of the three rays is most likely the light ray that travels in the air after emerging from the opposite side of the block?

_____

Sketch the path the light would take inside the glass.

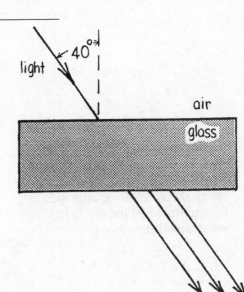

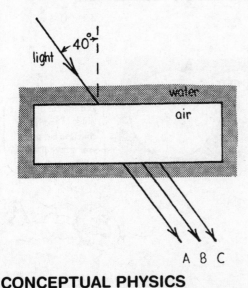

4. To the left, a light ray is shown moving from water into a rectangular block of air (inside a thin-walled plastic box) at 40° to the normal. Which of the three rays is most likely the light ray that continues into the water on the opposite side of the block?

_____

Sketch the path the light would take inside the air.

thanx to Clarence Bakken

CONCEPTUAL PHYSICS

5. The two transparent blocks (right) are made of different materials. The speed of light in the left block is greater than the speed of light in the right block. Draw an appropriate light path through and beyond the right block. Is the light that emerges displaced more or less than light emerging from the left block?

_____

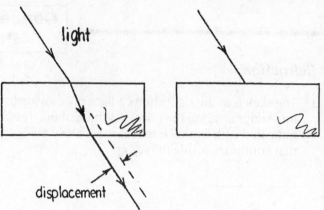

6. Light from the air passes through plates of glass and plastic below. The speeds of light in the different materials is shown to the right (these different speeds are often implied by the "index of refraction" of the material). Construct a rough sketch showing an appropriate path through the system of four plates.

Compared to the 50° incident ray at the top, what can you say about the angles of the ray in the air between and below the block pairs?

_____

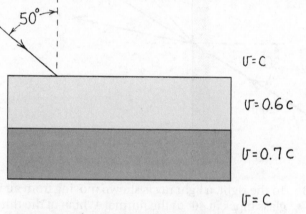

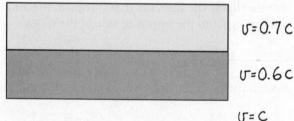

7. Parallel rays of light are refracted as they change speed in passing from air into the eye (left). Construct a rough sketch showing appropriate light paths when parallel light under water meets the same eye (right).

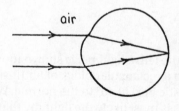

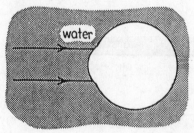

If a fish out of water wishes to clearly view objects in air, should it wear goggles filled with water or with air?

8. Why do we need to wear a face mask or goggles to see clearly when under water?

_____

CONCEPTUAL PHYSICS

Pool Room Optics

The law of reflection for optics is useful in playing pool. A ball bouncing off the bank of a pool table behaves like a photon reflecting off a mirror. As the sketch shows, angles become straight lines with the help of mirrors. The diagram shows a top view of this, with a flattened "mirrored" region. Note that the angled path on the table appears as a straight line (dashed) in the mirrored region.

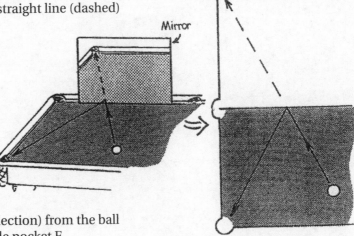

1. Consider a one-bank shot (one reflection) from the ball to the north bank and then into side pocket E.

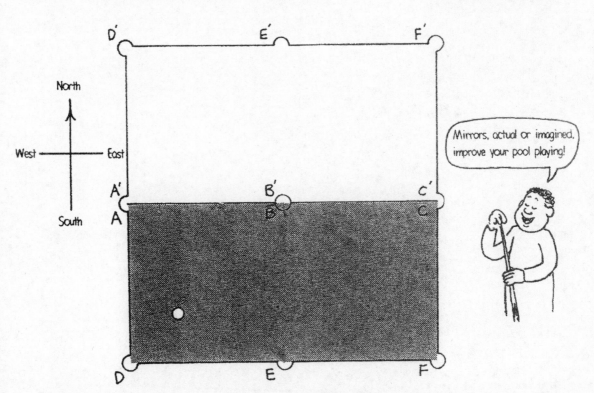

Mirrors, actual or imagined, improve your pool playing!

a. Use the mirror method to construct a straight line path to mirrored E'. Then construct the actual path to E.

b. Without using off-center strokes or other tricks, can a one-bank shot off the north bank put the ball in corner pocket F? _____ Show why or why not using the diagram.

CONCEPTUAL PHYSICS

Pinhole Image Formation

Look carefully at the round spots of light on the shady ground beneath trees. These are sunballs, and are actually images of the sun. They are cast by openings between leaves in the trees that act as pinholes. Large sunballs, several centimeters in diameter or so, are cast by openings that are relatively high above the ground, while small ones are produced by closer "pinholes." The interesting point is that the ratio of the diameter of the sunball to its distance from the pinhole is the same as the ratio of the sun's diameter to its distance from the pinhole. We know the sun is approximately 150,000,000 km from the pinhole, so careful measurement of this ratio tells us the diameter of the sun. That's what this page is about. Instead of finding sunballs under the shade of trees, make your own easier-to-measure sunballs.

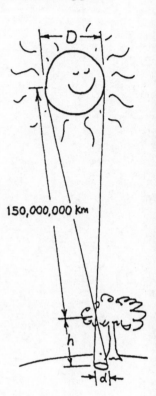

1. Poke a small hole in a piece of cardboard (like with a sharp pencil). Hold the cardboard in the sunlight and note the circular image that is cast. This is an image of the sun. Note that its size does not depend on the size of the hole in the cardboard, but only on its distance. The image will be a circle when cast on a surface that is perpendicular to the rays — otherwise it will be "stretched out" as an ellipse.

2. If you were doing this when the sun is partially eclipsed, what image shape would you expect to see? _____

3. Try holes of different shapes — say a square hole, or a triangular hole. What is the shape of the image when its distance from the cardboard is large compared to the size of the hole? _____ Does the shape of the "pinhole" make a difference?

   _____

4. Measure the diameter of a small coin. Then place the coin on a viewing area that is perpendicular to the sun's rays. Position the cardboard so the image exactly covers the coin. Carefully measure the distance between the coin and the the small hole in the cardboard. Complete the following:

   $$\frac{\text{Diameter of sunball}}{\text{Distance to pinhole}} = \text{_____}$$

   WHAT SHAPE DO SUNBALLS HAVE DURING A PARTIAL ECLIPSE OF THE SUN ?

   With this ratio, estimate the diameter of the sun. Show your work on the back.

CONCEPTUAL PHYSICS

Concept-Development Practice Page   30-2

Lenses

Rays of light bend as shown when passing through the glass blocks.

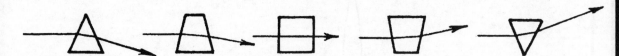

1. Show how light rays bend when they pass through the arrangement of glass blocks shown below.

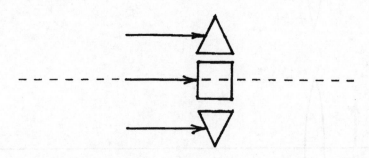

2. Show how light rays bend when they pass through the lens shown below. Is the lens a converging or a diverging lens? What is your evidence?

    _____
    _____

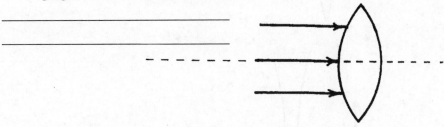

3. Show how light rays bend when they pass through the arrangement of glass blocks shown below.

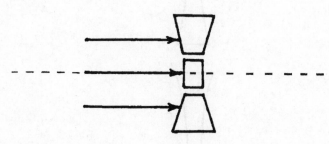

4. Show how light rays bend when they pass through the lens shown below. Is the lens a converging or a diverging lens? What is your evidence?

    _____
    _____

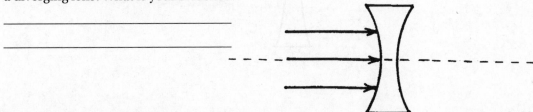

CONCEPTUAL PHYSICS

5. Which type of lens is used to correct farsightedness? _____

   Nearsightedness? _____

6. Use the ray-diagram technique (described in Section 30.3 of your text) to find the location and relative size of the arrow's image for each of the lenses below.

Concept-Development Practice Page · 31-1

Diffraction and Interference

1. Shown below are concentric solid and dashed circles, each different in radius by 1 cm. Consider the circular pattern of a top view of water waves, where the solid circles are crests and the dashed circles are troughs.

   a. Draw another set of the same concentric circles with a compass. Choose any part of the paper for your center (except the present central point). Let the circles run off the edge of the paper.

   b. Find where a dashed line crosses a solid line and draw a large dot at the intersection. Do this for ALL places where a solid and dashed line intersect.

   c. With a wide felt marker, connect the dots with smooth lines. These *nodal lines* lie in regions where the waves have canceled — where the crest of one wave overlaps the trough of another (see Figures 25.11 and 31.12 in the textbook).

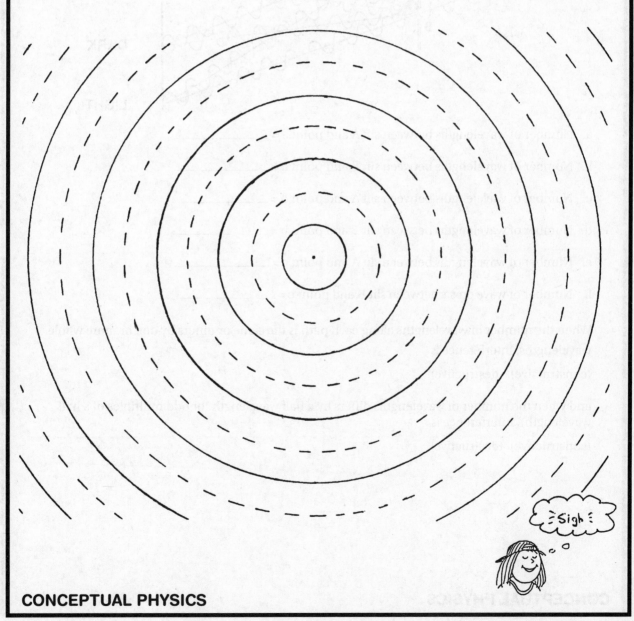

CONCEPTUAL PHYSICS

2. Look at the construction of overlapping circles on your classmates' papers. Some will have more nodal lines than others, due to different starting points. How does the number of nodal lines in a pattern relate to the distance between the centers of the circles (or sources of waves)?

_____

_____

3. Figure 31.15 from your text is repeated below. Carefully count the number of wavelengths (same as the number of wave crests) along the following paths between the slits and the screen.

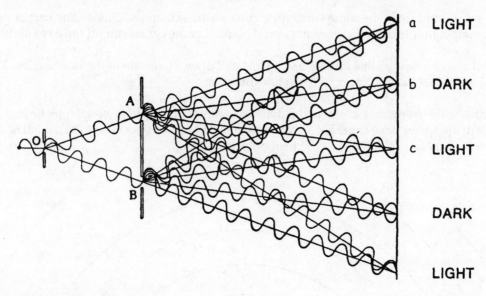

a. Number of wavelengths between slit A and point a = _____

b. Number of wavelengths between slit B and point a = _____

c. Number of wavelengths between slit A and point b = _____

d. Number of wavelengths between slit B and point b = _____

e. Number of wavelengths between slit A and point c = _____

f. Number of wave crests between slit B and point c = _____

When the number of wavelengths along each path is the same or differs by one or more whole wavelengths, interference is

(constructive) (destructive)

and when the number of wavelengths differs by a half wavelength (or odd multiples of a half wavelength), interference is

(constructive) (destructive).

CONCEPTUAL PHYSICS

Concept-Development Practice Page | 32-1

Coulomb's Law

1. The diagram is of a hydrogen atom.

   a. Label the proton in the nucleus with a + sign and the orbital electron with a – sign.

   b. The electrical interaction between the nucleus and the orbital electron is a force of

   (attraction) (repulsion).

   c. According to Coulomb's law,

   $$F = k\frac{q_1 q_2}{d^2}$$

   if the charge of either the nucleus or the orbital electron were greater, the force between the nucleus and the electron would be

   (greater) (less)

   and if the distance between the nucleus and electron were greater the force would be
   (greater) (less).

   If the distance between the nucleus and electron were doubled, the force would be

   (1/4 as much) (1/2 as much) (two times as much) (4 times as much).

2. Consider the electric force between a pair of charged particles a certain distance apart. By Coulomb's law:

   a. If the charge on one of the particles is doubled, the force is

   (unchanged) (halved) (doubled) (quadrupled).

   b. If instead the charge on both particles is doubled, the force is

   (unchanged) (halved) (doubled) (quadrupled).

   c. If instead the distance between the particles is halved, the force is

   (unchanged) (halved) (doubled) (quadrupled).

   d. If the distance is halved, *and* the charge of both particles is doubled,
   the force is _____ times as great.

CONCEPTUAL PHYSICS

Electrostatics

1. The outer electrons in metals are not tightly bound to the atomic nuclei. They are free to roam in the material. Such materials are good

   (conductors) (insulators).

   Electrons in other materials are tightly bound to the atomic nuclei, and are not free to roam in the material. These materials are good

   (conductors) (insulators).

2. A rubber rod that has been rubbed with fur is negatively charged because rubber holds electrons better than fur does. When the rod touches a metal sphere, some of the charge from the rod spreads onto the metal sphere because like charges repel one another. When the rod is removed the charge spreads evenly over the metal sphere and remains there because the insulating stand prevents its flow to the ground. The negatively charged rod has given the sphere a negative charge. This is *charging by contact*, and is shown to the right.

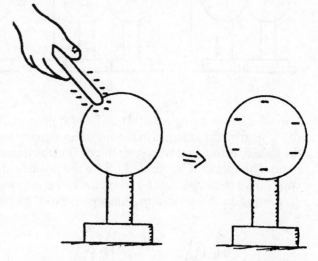

   Label the right-hand sphere below with the appropriate charges below for a positively-charged rod touching a metal sphere.

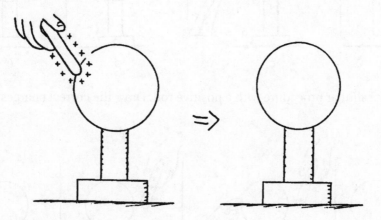

3. In the examples above, electric charge is

   (created from nothing) (simply transferred from one body to another).

4. A positively-charged balloon will stick to a wooden wall. It does this by polarizing molecules in the wooden wall to create an oppositely-charged surface. Draw the appropriate charges on both the balloon and in the wall. Your completed diagram should be similar to Figure 32.13 in your textbook.

CONCEPTUAL PHYSICS

5. Consider the diagrams below. (a) A pair of insulated metal spheres, A and B, touch each other, so in effect they form a single uncharged conductor. (b) A positively charged rod is brought near A, but not touching, and electrons in the metal sphere are attracted toward the rod. Charges in the spheres have redistributed, and the negative charge is labeled. Draw the appropriate + signs that are repelled to the far side of B. Draw the signs of charge in (c), when the spheres are separated while the rod is still present, and in (d) after the rod has been removed. Your completed work should be similar to Figure 32.8 in the textbook. The spheres have been charged by *induction*.

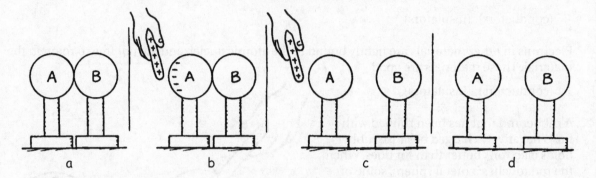

6. Consider below a single metal insulated sphere, (a), initially uncharged. When a negatively charged rod is nearby, (b), charges in the metal are separated. Electrons are repelled to the far side. When the sphere is touched with your finger, (c), electrons flow out to the sphere to Earth through the hand. The sphere is "grounded." Note the positive charge left (d) while the rod is still present and your finger removed, and (e) when the rod is removed. This is an example of *charge induction by grounding*. In this procedure the negative rod "gives" a positive charge to the sphere.

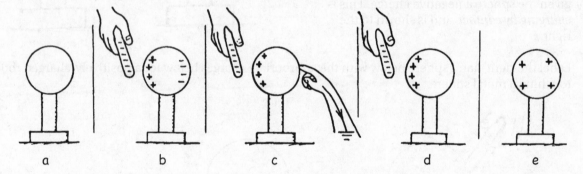

The diagrams below show a similar procedure with a positive rod. Draw the correct charges in the diagrams.

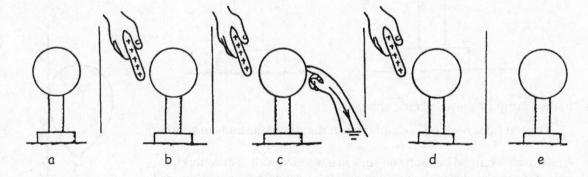

Concept-Development Practice Page | 33-1

Electric Field

1. An *electric field* surrounds an electric charge. The field strength at any place in the field can be found by placing a small positive test charge there. Where the force on the test charge is great, the field strength is great; where the force is weak, the field strength is weak. Electric field strength is directly proportional to the force exerted on a positive test charge.

   The direction of an electric field at any point is the same as the direction of the force exerted on the positive test charge.

   Some electric field lines surrounding a positive charge are shown above. They extend radially from the charge. A vector is sketched at point *a* to represent the force that would be exerted on a positive test charge there (its direction shows that like charges repel). Other points *b, c, d, e* and *f,* are all located at the same distance from the positive charge.

   Draw a vector at each of the points *b – f* to show the force on the same test charge.

2. The electric field about a negative charge is shown to the right. The field lines point radially inward, in the same direction a positive test charge would be forced. Assume the magnitude of the negative charge is the same as the charge above.

   Draw field vectors at each of the points *h – m.*

3. The pair of equal and opposite charges of Questions 1 and 2 is shown below. Their individual fields, drawn uninfluenced by each other, overlap to form a field pattern that can be constructed by vector rules. This is shown at locations *a* and *b,* where the two forces combine to a single resultant force. Note that point *b* overlaps point *m,* and also points *c* and *l* overlap. Note how the size of each vector depends on its distance from the charge (inverse-square law). Every point in the field is the result of both the positive and the negative charges.

   By vector rules, show the resultant of all the vector pairs shown. Then sketch in sample vector resultants at a few other places. Does the pattern that emerges agree with the field patterns shown in Figure a on the next page? _____

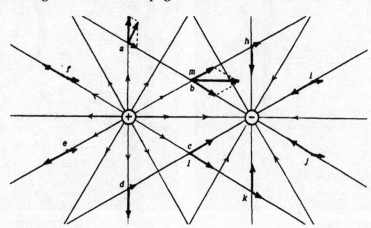

4. A copy of Figure 33.5 in your textbook is shown below. Three points, (*a*, *b*, *c*), are indicated on each electric field pattern. Point *a* in each pattern shows the electric field vector at that point. The vector indicates the magnitude and direction of the force that a positive test charge would experience at that point. (A curved field indicates that the force on a nearby test charge would be different in magnitude and direction.) Use the vector at points *a* as a reference and sketch in the electric field vectors for points *b* and *c* in each pattern, using colored ink or pencil.

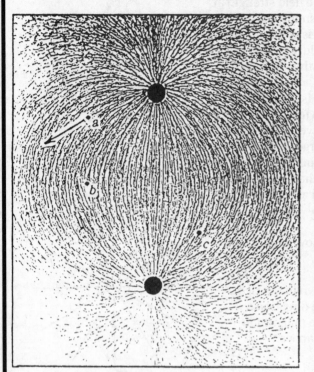

a. Equal and opposite charges

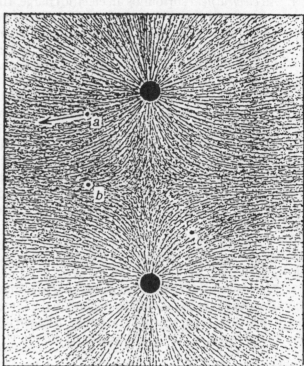

b. Equal like charges

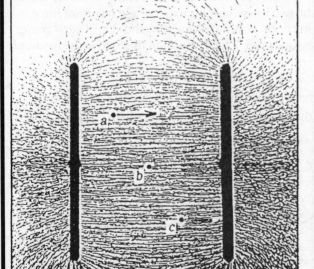

c. Oppositely charged plates

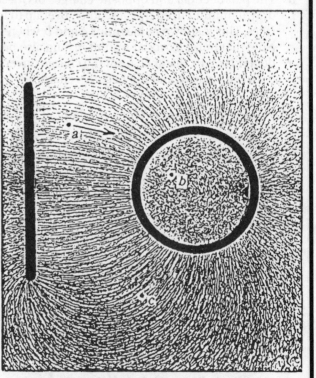

d. Oppositely charged plate and cylinder

CONCEPTUAL PHYSICS

Concept-Development Practice Page · 33-2

Electric Potential

1.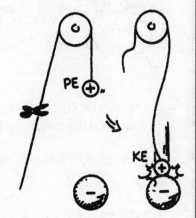

Just as PE (potential energy) transforms to KE (kinetic energy) for a mass lifted against the gravitational field (left), the electric PE of an electric charge transforms to other forms of energy when it changes location in an electric field (right). When released, how does the KE acquired by each compare to the decrease in PE?

_____

2. *Complete the statements.*

A force compresses the spring. The work done in compression is the product of the average force and the distance moved. $W = Fd$. This work increases the PE of the spring.

Similarly, a force pushes the charge (call it a test charge) closer to the charged sphere. The work done in moving the test charge is the product of the average _____ and the _____ moved.
$W =$ _____. This work _____ the PE of the test charge.

If the test charge is released, it will be repelled and fly past the starting point. Its gain in KE at this point is _____ to its decrease in PE.

At any point, a greater quantity of test charge means a greater amount of PE, but not a greater amount of PE *per quantity* of charge. The quantities of PE (measured in joules) and PE/charge (measured in volts) are different concepts.

By definition: **Electric Potential = PE/charge.** 1 volt = 1 joule/1 coulomb

3. *Complete the statements.*

ELECTRIC PE/CHARGE HAS THE SPECIAL NAME *ELECTRIC* _____

SINCE IT IS MEASURED IN *VOLTS* IT IS COMMONLY CALLED _____

CONCEPTUAL PHYSICS

4. When a charge of 1 C has an electric PE of 1 J, it has an electric potential of 1 V. When a charge of 2 C has an electric PE of 2 J, its potential is _____ V.

5. If a conductor connected to the terminal of a battery has a potential of 12 volts, then each coulomb of charge on the conductor has a PE of _____ J.

6. If a charge of 1 C has a PE of 5000 J, its voltage is _____ V.

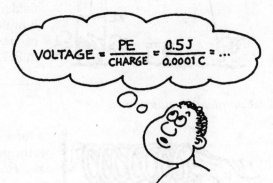

7. If a charge of 0.001 C has a PE of 5 J, its voltage is _____ V.

8. If a charge of 0.0001 C has a PE of 0.5 J, its voltage is _____ V.

9. If a rubber balloon is charged to 5000 V, and the quantity of charge on the balloon is 1 millionth coulomb, (0.000001 C) then the PE of this charge is only _____ J.

10. Some people get mixed up between force and pressure. Recall that pressure is force *per area*. Similarly, some people get mixed up between electric PE and voltage. According to this chapter, voltage is electric PE *per* _____.

ELECTRIC POTENTIAL IS NOT THE SAME AS ELECTRIC POTENTIAL ENERGY (PE). VOLTAGE AND ELECTRIC POTENTIAL ARE THE SAME. WE'LL SEE IN THE NEXT CHAPTER THEY ARE A SORT OF "ELECTRIC PRESSURE."

CONCEPTUAL PHYSICS

Electric Current

1. Water doesn't flow in the pipe when (a) both ends are at the same level. Another way of saying this is that water will not flow in the pipe when both ends have the same potential energy (PE). Similarly, charge will not flow in a conductor if both ends of the conductor are at the same electric potential. But tip the water pipe and increase the PE of one side so there is a difference in PE across the ends of the pipe, as in (b), and water will flow. Similarly, increase the electric potential of one end of an electric conductor so there is a potential difference across the ends, and charge will flow.

a. The units of electric potential difference are

(volts) (amperes) (ohms) (watts).

b. It is common to call electric potential difference

(voltage) (amperage) (wattage).

c. The flow of electric charge is called electric

(voltage) (current) (power),

and is measured in

(volts) (amperes) (ohms) (watts).

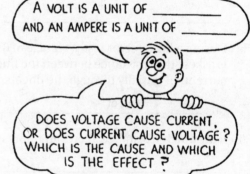

A VOLT IS A UNIT OF _____ AND AN AMPERE IS A UNIT OF _____

DOES VOLTAGE CAUSE CURRENT, OR DOES CURRENT CAUSE VOLTAGE? WHICH IS THE CAUSE AND WHICH IS THE EFFECT?

2. *Complete the statements.*

a. A current of 1 ampere is a flow of charge at the rate of ____1____ coulomb per second.

b. When a charge of 15 C flows through any area in a circuit each second, the current is ___15___ A.

c. One volt is the potential difference between two points if 1 joule of energy is needed to move

____1____ coulomb of charge between the two points.

d. When a lamp is plugged into a 120-V socket, each coulomb of charge that flows in the current is

raised to a potential energy of ___120___ joules.

e. Which offers more resistance to water flow, a wide pipe or a narrow pipe? ___wide___

Similarly, which offers more resistance to the flow of charge, a thick wire or a thin wire?

___thin___

CONCEPTUAL PHYSICS

Ohm's Law

1. How much current flows in a 1000-ohm resistor when 1.5 volts are impressed across it?

   0.0015   A

2. If the filament resistance in an automobile headlamp is 3 ohms, how many amps does it draw when connected to a 12-volt battery?

   4 A

3. The resistance of the side lights on an automobile are 10 ohms. How much current flows in them when connected to 12 volts?

   1.2   A

4. What is the current in the 30-ohm heating coil of a coffee maker that operates on a 120-volt circuit?

   4   A

5. During a lie detector test, a voltage of 6 V is impressed across two fingers. When a certain question is asked, the resistance between the fingers drops from 400,000 ohms to 200,000 ohms. What is the current (a) initially through the fingers, and (b) when the resistance between them drops?

   (a) _____ 0.000015 _____ A   (b) _____ 0.00003 _____ A

6. How much resistance allows an impressed voltage of 6 V to produce a current of 0.006 A?

   1000   Ω

7. What is the resistance of a clothes iron that draws a current of 12 A at 120 V?

   10   Ω

8. What is the voltage across a 100-ohm circuit element that draws a current of 1 A?

   100   V

9. What voltage will produce 3 A through a 15-ohm resistor?

   45   V

OHM MY GOODNESS!

10. The current in an incandescent lamp is 0.5 A when connected to a 120-V circuit, and 0.2 A when connected to a 10-V source. Does the resistance of the lamp change in these cases? Explain your answer and defend it with numerical values.

   Yes

   _____

   _____

   _____

CONCEPTUAL PHYSICS

Name _Colm Keating_ Class _____ Date _____

Electric Power

Recall that the rate energy is converted from one form to another is *power.*

$$\text{power} = \frac{\text{energy converted}}{\text{time}} = \frac{\text{voltage} \times \text{charge}}{\text{time}} = \text{voltage} \times \frac{\text{charge}}{\text{time}} = \text{voltage} \times \text{current}$$

The unit of power is the *watt* (or *kilowatt).* So in units form,

Electric power (*watts*) = current (*amperes*) × voltage (*volts),*

where 1 *watt* = 1 *ampere* × 1 *volt.*

THAT'S RIGHT··· VOLTAGE = $\frac{ENERGY}{CHARGE}$, SO ENERGY = VOLTAGE × CHARGE ··· AND $\frac{CHARGE}{TIME}$ = CURRENT ⸴ NEAT ⸴

A 100-WATT BULB CONVERTS ELECTRIC ENERGY INTO HEAT AND LIGHT MORE QUICKLY THAN A 25-WATT BULB. THAT'S WHY FOR THE SAME VOLTAGE A 100-WATT BULB GLOWS BRIGHTER THAN A 25-WATT BULB!

1. What is the power when a voltage of 120 V drives a 2-A current through a device?

   _240 w_

2. What is the current when a 60-W lamp is connected to 120 V?

   _½ A_

WHICH DRAWS MORE CURRENT ··· THE 100-WATT OR THE 25-WATT BULB?

3. How much current does a 100-W lamp draw when connected to 120 V?

   _0.3 A_

4. If part of an electric circuit dissipates energy at 6 W when it draws a current of 3 A, what voltage is impressed across it?

   _2 V_

5. The equation $\text{power} = \frac{\text{energy converted}}{\text{time}}$

   rearranged gives   energy converted = _(power)(Time)_

WATT'S HAPPENING?

6. Explain the difference between a kilowatt and a kilowatt-hour.

   _____

7. One deterrent to burglary is to leave your front porch light on all the time. If your fixture contains a 60-W bulb at 120 V, and your local power utility sells energy at 8 cents per kilowatt-hour, how much will it cost to leave the bulb on for the whole month? Show your work on the other side of this page.

CONCEPTUAL PHYSICS

Concept-Development Practice Page 35-1

Series Circuits

1. In the circuit shown at the right, a voltage of 6 V pushes charge through a single resistor of 2 Ω. According to Ohm's law, the current in the resistor (and therefore in the whole circuit) is _____ A.

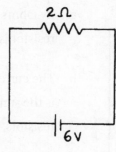

THE EQUIVALENT RESISTANCE OF RESISTORS IN SERIES IS SIMPLY THEIR SUM!

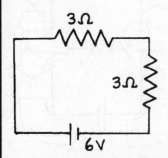

2. If a second identical lamp is added, as on the left, the 6-V battery must push charge through a total resistance of _____ Ω. The current in the circuit is then _____ A.

3. The equivalent resistance of three 4-Ω resistors in series is _____ Ω.

4. Does current flow *through* a resistor, or *across* a resistor? _____

   Is voltage established *through* a resistor, or *across* a resistor? _____

5. Does current in the lamps occur simultaneously, or does charge flow first through one lamp, then the other, and finally the last in turn?

   _____

6. Circuits (a) and (b) below are identical with all bulbs rated at equal wattage (therefore equal resistance). The only difference between the circuits is that Bulb 5 has a short circuit, as shown.

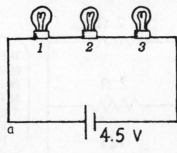

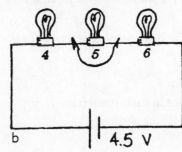

   a. In which circuit is the current greater? _____

   b. In which circuit are all three bulbs equally bright? _____

   c. What bulbs are the brightest? _____

   d. What bulb is the dimmest? _____

   e. What bulbs have the largest voltage drops across them? _____

   f. Which circuit dissipates more power? _____

   g. What circuit produces more light? _____

CONCEPTUAL PHYSICS

Parallel Circuits

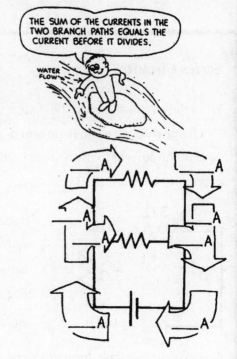

1. In the circuit shown below, there is a voltage drop of 6 V across *each* 2-Ω resistor.

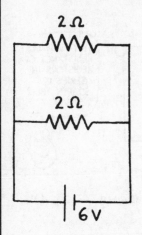

   a. By Ohm's law, the current in *each* resistor is _____ A.

   b. The current through the battery is the sum of the currents in the resistors, _____ A.

   c. Fill in the current in the eight blank spaces in the view of the *same circuit* shown again at the right.

2. Cross out the circuit below that is *not* equivalent to the circuit above.

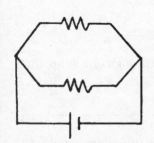 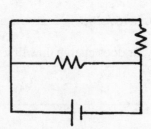 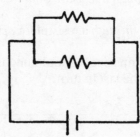 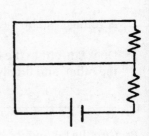

3. Consider the parallel circuit at the right.

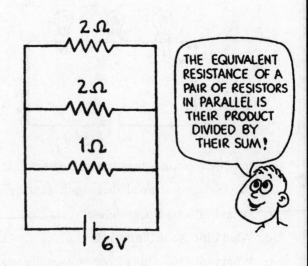

   a. The voltage drop across each resistor is _____ V.

   b. The current in each branch is:

   2-Ω resistor _____A

   2-Ω resistor _____A

   1-Ω resistor _____A

   b. The current through the battery equals the sum of the currents which equals _____ A.

   c. The equivalent resistance of the circuit equals _____ Ω.

CONCEPTUAL PHYSICS

Compound Circuits

1. The initial circuit, below left, is a compound circuit made of a combination of resistors. It is reduced to a single equivalent resistance by the three steps, the circuits to its right, (a), (b), (c). In step (a), show the equivalent resistance of the parallel 4-Ω resistors. In step (b), combine this in series with the 3-Ω resistor. In step *c*, combine the last parallel pair to obtain the equivalent resistance of the circuit. (Note the similarity of this circuit and Figure 35.10 in your textbook.)

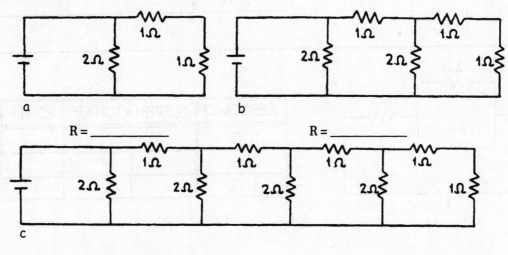

Initial Circuit   a   b   c

2. The circuit below is similar to Figure 35.11 in your textbook. In three successive steps, as in Question 1, replace each pair of resistors by a single resistor of equivalent resistance.

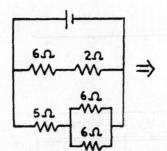

R = _____

3. Find the equivalent resistance of these three circuits.

a

b

R = _____   R = _____

c

R = _____

CONCEPTUAL PHYSICS

4. The table beside circuit (a) below shows the current through each resistor, the voltage across each resistor, and the power dissipated as heat in each resistor. Find the similar correct values for circuits (b), (c), and (d), and put your answers in the tables shown.

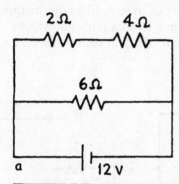

RESISTANCE	CURRENT ×	VOLTAGE =	POWER
2 Ω	2 A	4 V	8 W
4 Ω	2 A	8 V	16 W
6 Ω	2 A	12 V	24 W

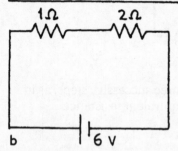

RESISTANCE	CURRENT ×	VOLTAGE =	POWER
1 Ω			
2 Ω			

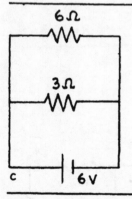

RESISTANCE	CURRENT ×	VOLTAGE =	POWER
6 Ω			
3 Ω			

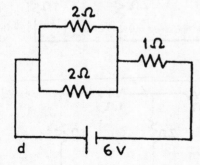

RESISTANCE	CURRENT ×	VOLTAGE =	POWER
2 Ω			
2 Ω			
1 Ω			

CONCEPTUAL PHYSICS

Circuit Resistance

All circuits below have the same lamp A with resistance of 6 Ω, and the same 12-volt battery with negligible resistance. The unknown resistances of lamps B through L are such that the current in lamp A remains 1 ampere. *Fill in the blanks.*

Figure what the resistances are, then show their values in the blanks to the left of each lamp.

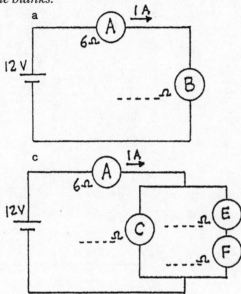

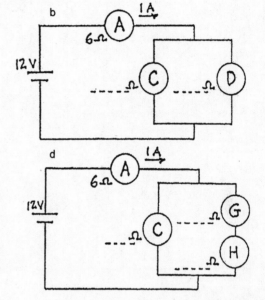

Circuit a: How much current flows through the battery? _____ A

Circuit b: Assume lamps C and D are identical. Current through lamp D is

_____ A.

Circuit c: Identical lamps E and F replace lamp D.

Current through lamp C is _____ A.

Circuit d: Lamps G and H replace lamps E and F, and the resistance of lamp G is twice that of lamp H. Current through

lamp H is _____ A.

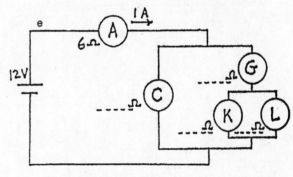

Handy rule: For a pair of resistors in parallel:

Equivalent resistance = $\dfrac{\text{product of resistances}}{\text{sum of resistances}}$

Circuit e: Identical lamps K and L replace lamp H. Current through lamp L is _____ A.

The equivalent resistance of a circuit is the value of a single resistor that will replace all the resistors of the circuit to produce the same load on the battery. How do the equivalent resistances of the circuits a through e compare?

_____

CONCEPTUAL PHYSICS

Magnetism

Fill in each blank with the appropriate word.

1. Attraction or repulsion of charges depends on their *signs*, positives or negatives. Attraction or repulsion of magnets depends on their magnetic _____,

   _____ or _____ .

2. Opposite poles attract; like poles _____.

3. A magnetic field is produced by the _____ of electric charge.

4. Clusters of magnetically aligned atoms are magnetic _____.

5. A magnetic _____ surrounds a current-carrying wire.

6. When a current-carrying wire is made to form a coil around a piece of iron, the result is an

   _____.

7. A charged particle moving in a magnetic field experiences a deflecting _____ that is maximum when the charge moves

   _____ to the field.

8. A current-carrying wire experiences a deflecting

   _____ that is maximum when the wire

   and magnetic field are _____ to one another.

9. A simple instrument designed to detect electric current is the _____ ; when calibrated to measure current, it is an _____; when calibrated to measure voltage, it is a _____ .

10. The largest size magnet in the world is the

    _____ itself.

CONCEPTUAL PHYSICS

11. The illlustration below is similar to Figure 36.4 in your textbook. Iron filings trace out patterns of magnetic field lines about a bar magnet. In the field are some magnetic compasses. The compass needle in only one compass is shown. Draw in the needles with proper orientation in the other compasses.

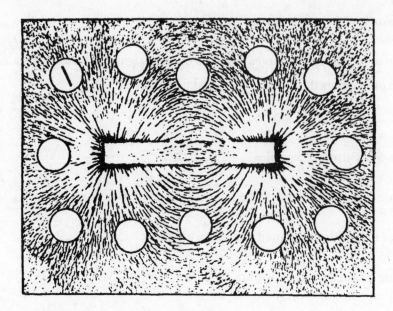

12. The illustration below is similar to Figure 36.13 (center) in your textbook. Iron filings trace out the magnetic field pattern about the loop of current-carrying wire. Draw in the compass needle orientations for all the compasses.

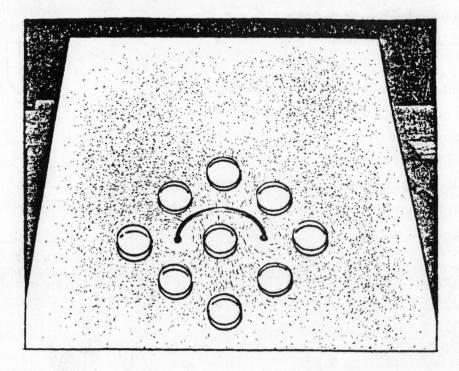

CONCEPTUAL PHYSICS

Concept-Development Practice Page 37-1

Faraday's Law

1. Hans Christian Oersted discovered that magnetism and electricity are

    (related) (independent of each other).

    Magnetism is produced by

    (batteries) (the motion of electric charges).

Faraday and Henry discovered that electric current can be produced by

(batteries) (motion of a magnet).

More specifically, voltage is induced in a loop of wire if there is a change in the

(batteries) (magnetic field in the loop).

This phenomenon is called

(electromagnetism) (electromagnetic induction).

2. When a magnet is plunged in and out of a coil of wire, voltage is induced in the coil. If the rate of the in-and-out motion of the magnet is doubled, the induced voltage

    (doubles) (halves) (remains the same).

    If instead the number of loops in the coil is doubled, the induced voltage

    (doubles) (halves) (remains the same).

3. A rapidly changing magnetic field in any region of space induces a rapidly changing

    (electric field) (magnetic field) (gravitational field)

    which in turn induces a rapidly changing

    (magnetic field) (electric field) (baseball field).

    This generation and regeneration of electric and magnetic fields makes up

    (electromagnetic waves) (sound waves) (both of these).

CONCEPTUAL PHYSICS

Transformers

Consider a simple transformer that has a 100-turn primary coil and a 1000-turn secondary coil. The primary is connected to a 120-V AC source and the secondary is connected to an electrical device with a resistance of 1000 ohms.

1. What will be the voltage output of the secondary?

   _____ V

2. What current flows in the secondary circuit? _____ A

3. Now that you know the voltage and the current, what is the power

   in the secondary coil? _____ W

4. Neglecting small heating losses, and knowing that energy is conserved, what is the power

   in the primary coil? _____ W

5. Now that you know the power and the voltage across the primary coil, what is the current drawn by

   the primary coil? _____ A

Circle the correct answers.

6. The results show voltage is stepped (up) (down) from primary to secondary, and that current is

   correspondingly stepped (up) (down).

7. For a step-up transformer, there are (more) (fewer) turns in the secondary coil than the primary.

   For such a transformer, there is (more) (less) current in the secondary than in the primary.

8. A transformer can step up (voltage) (energy and power), but in no way can it step up

   (voltage) (energy and power).

9. If 120 V is used to power a toy electric train that operates on 6 V, then a (step up) (step down)

   transformer should be used that has a primary to secondary turns ratio of (1/20) (20/1).

10. A transformer operates on (DC) (AC) because the magnetic field within the iron core

    must (continually change) (remain steady).

Power Transmission

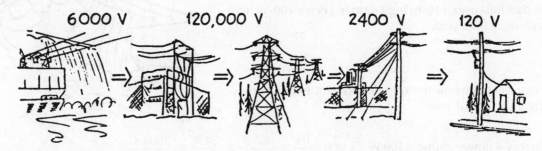

6000 V   120,000 V   2400 V   120 V

Many power companies provide power to cities that are far from the generators. Consider a city of 100,000 persons who each continually use 120 W of power (equivalent to the operation of two 60-W light bulbs per person). The power constantly consumed is 100,000 persons × 120 W / 1 person = 12 million W (12 MW).

1. What current corresponds to this amount of power at the common 120 V used by consumers?

$$P = IV$$
$$12,000,000 \text{ W} = I \times 120 \text{ V}$$
$$I = \frac{\text{W}}{\text{V}} = \underline{\hspace{2cm}} \text{A}$$

PHYSICS SIGH

This is an enormous current, more than can be carried in the thickest of wires without overheating. More power would be dissipated in the form of heat than would reach the faraway city. Fortunately the important quantity is *IV* and not *I* alone. Power companies transmit power over long distances at very high voltages so that the current in the wires is low and heating of the power lines is minimized.

2. If the 12 MW of power is transmitted at 120,000 V, the current in the wires is

$$I = \frac{P}{V} = \frac{\text{W}}{\text{V}} = \underline{\hspace{2cm}} \text{A}$$

This amount of current can be carried in long-distance power lines with only small power losses due to heating (normally less than 1%). But the corresponding high voltages wired to houses would be very dangerous. So step-down transformers are used in the city.

3. What ratio of primary turns to secondary turns should be on a transformer to step 120,000 V down to 2400 V? _____

4. What ratio of primary turns to secondary turns should be on a transformer to step 2400 V down to 120 V used in household circuits? _____

5. What is the main benefit of AC compared to DC power?

_____

_____

CONCEPTUAL PHYSICS

Power Production

Does it take a lot of water to light a light bulb? That depends on its wattage and how long it glows. In this practice page, you are to calculate the mass and volume of water that falls over a 10-m high dam to keep a 100-W light bulb glowing for 1 year.

USE YOUR CALCULATOR WITH THIS ONE!

1. First, calculate how many joules are required to keep the bulb lit for 1 year.

$$\text{Energy} = \text{power} \times \text{time} = 100 \, \cancel{W} \times 1 \, \cancel{yr} \times \frac{1 \, \text{J/s}}{1 \, \cancel{W}} \times \frac{365 \, \cancel{d}}{1 \, \cancel{yr}} \times \frac{24 \, \cancel{h}}{1 \, \cancel{d}} \times \frac{3600 \, \cancel{s}}{1 \, \cancel{h}}$$

$$= \underline{\hspace{2cm}} \, \text{J}$$

2. What mass of water elevated 10 m has this much PE? From Chapter 9, recall that gravitational PE = *mgh:*

$$\text{PE} = mgh$$

$$m = \frac{\text{PE}}{gh} = \frac{\underline{\hspace{2cm}}}{(9.8 \, \text{m/s}^2)(10 \, \text{m})} = \underline{\hspace{2cm}} \, \text{kg}$$

3. But this assumes 100% efficiency. A hydroelectric plant is typically 20% efficient. This means only 1 part in 5 of the PE of the falling water ends up as electricity. So the mass above must be multiplied by 5 to get the actual amount of water that must fall to keep the 100-W bulb lit.

$$5 \times \underline{\hspace{2cm}} \, \text{kg} = \underline{\hspace{2cm}} \, \text{kg}$$

4. This is an impressive number of kilograms! To visualize this amount of water, convert it to cubic meters. (Recall 1 kg of water occupies 1 liter, and there are 1000 liters in 1 cubic meter.)

$$\text{Volume} = \underline{\hspace{2cm}} \, \cancel{kg} \times 1 \, \frac{\cancel{L}}{\cancel{kg}} \times \frac{1 \, \text{m}^3}{1000 \, \cancel{L}} = \underline{\hspace{2cm}} \, \text{m}^3$$

5. For comparison, an Olympic-size swimming pool holds about 4000 m^3 of water. How many such poolfuls of water are required to keep a 100-W bulb lit for one year?

$$\text{Number of poolfuls} = \frac{\underline{\hspace{2cm}} \, \cancel{m^3}}{\underline{\hspace{1cm}} \, \cancel{m^3}/\text{poolful}} \approx \underline{\hspace{1cm}} \, \text{poolfuls}$$

Does it take a lot of water to light a light bulb? To light a city full of light bulbs? Now you have a better idea!

Concept-Development Practice Page 38-1

The Atom and the Quantum

1. To say that light is quantized means that light is made up of

   (elemental units) (waves).

2. Compared to photons of low-frequency light, photons of higher-frequency light have more

   (energy) (speed) (quanta).

3. The photoelectric effect supports the

   (wave model of light) (particle model of light).

4. The photoelectric effect is evident when light shone on certain photosensitive materials ejects

   (photons) (electrons).

5. 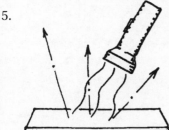 The photoelectric effect is more effective with violet light than with red light because the photons of violet light

   (resonate with the atoms in the material)

   (deliver more energy to the material)

   (are more numerous).

6. According to de Broglie's wave model of matter, a beam of light and a beam of electrons

   (are fundamentally different) (are similar).

7. According to de Broglie, the greater the speed of an electron beam, the

   (greater is its wavelength) (shorter is its wavelength).

8. The discreteness of the energy levels of electrons about the atomic nucleus is best understood by considering the electron to be a

   (wave) (particle).

9. Heavier atoms are not appreciably larger in size than lighter atoms. The main reason for this is the greater nuclear charge

   (pulls surrounding electrons into tighter orbits)

   (holds more electrons about the atomic nucleus) (produces a denser atomic structure).

10. Whereas in the everyday macroworld the study of motion is called *mechanics*, in the microworld the study of quanta is called

    (Newtonian mechanics) (quantum mechanics).

CONCEPTUAL PHYSICS

A QUANTUM MECHANIC!

**Concept-Development
Practice Page** **39-1**

The Atomic Nucleus and Radioactivity

1. *Complete the following statements.*

   a. A lone neutron spontaneously decays into a proton plus an

   _____.

   PHYSICS
   ≡SIGH≡

   b. Alpha and beta rays are made of streams of particles, whereas gamma

   rays are streams of _____.

   c. An electrically charged atom is called an _____.

   d. Different _____ of an element are chemically identical

   but differ in the number of neutrons in the nucleus.

   e. Transuranic elements are those beyond atomic number _____.

   f. If the amount of a certain radioactive sample decreases by half in four weeks, in four more

   weeks the amount remaining should be _____ the original amount.

   g. Water from a natural hot spring is warmed by _____ inside Earth.

2. The gas in the little girl's balloon is made up of former alpha
   and beta particles produced by radioactive decay.

   a. If the mixture is electrically neutral, how many more beta
   particles than alpha particles are in the balloon?

   _____

   _____

   b. Why is your answer not "same"?

   _____

   _____

   c. Why are the alpha and beta particles no longer harmful to the child?

   _____

   _____

   d. What element does this mixture make?

   _____

CONCEPTUAL PHYSICS

Radioactive Half-Life

You and your classmates will now play the "half-life game."
Each of you should have a coin to shake inside cupped
hands. After it has been shaken for a few seconds, the coin
is tossed on the table or on the floor. Students with tails
up fall out of the game. Only those who consistently show
heads remain in the game. Finally everybody has tossed a
tail and the game is over.

1. On the graph below, plot the number of students left in the game after each toss. Draw a
   smooth curve that passes close to the points on your plot. What is the similarity of your curve with
   that shown in Figure 39.13 of your textbook?

   _____

   _____

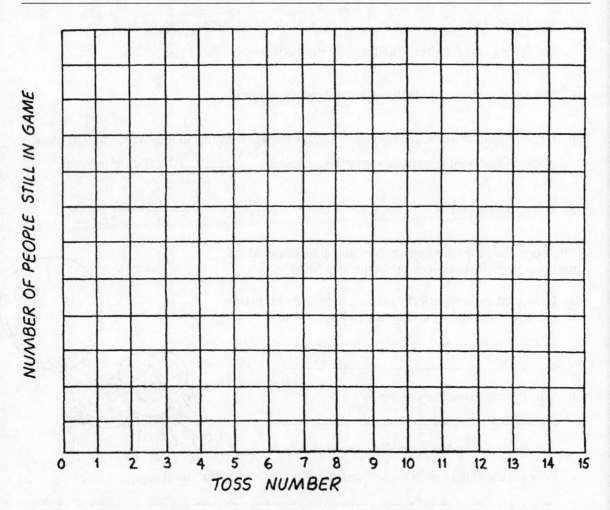

2. Was the person to last longest in the game *lucky*, with some sort of special powers to guide the long
   survival? What test could you make to decide the answer to this question?

   _____

   _____

CONCEPTUAL PHYSICS

Concept-Development Practice Page **39-2**

Natural Transmutation

Fill in the decay-scheme diagram below, similar to that shown on page 794 in the textbook, but beginning with U-235 and ending up with an isotope of lead. Use the table at the left, and identify each element in the series with its chemical symbol.

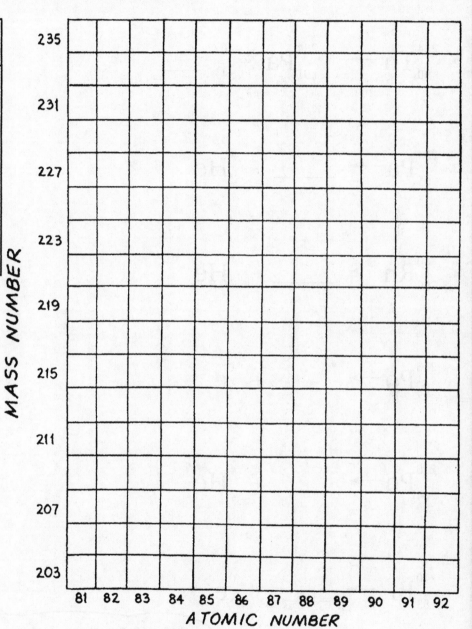

Step	Particle emitted
1	Alpha
2	Beta
3	Alpha
4	Alpha
5	Beta
6	Alpha
7	Alpha
8	Alpha
9	Beta
10	Alpha
11	Beta
12	Stable

MASS NUMBER

ATOMIC NUMBER

What isotope is the final product? _____

CONCEPTUAL PHYSICS

Nuclear Reactions

Complete these nuclear reactions.

1. $^{238}_{92}\text{U} \longrightarrow \ ^{234}_{90}\text{Th} + \ ^{4}_{2}\underline{\hspace{2cm}}$

2. $^{234}_{90}\text{Th} \longrightarrow \ ^{234}_{91}\text{Pa} + \ ^{0}_{-1}\underline{\hspace{1.5cm}}$

3. $^{234}_{91}\text{Pa} \longrightarrow \underline{\hspace{2cm}} + \ ^{4}_{2}\text{He}$

4. $^{220}_{86}\text{Rn} \longrightarrow \underline{\hspace{2cm}} + \ ^{4}_{2}\text{He}$

5. $^{216}_{84}\text{Po} \longrightarrow \underline{\hspace{2cm}} + \ ^{0}_{-1}\text{e}$

6. $^{216}_{84}\text{Po} \longrightarrow \underline{\hspace{2cm}} + \ ^{4}_{2}\text{He}$

7. $^{210}_{83}\text{Bi} \longrightarrow \underline{\hspace{2cm}} + \ ^{0}_{-1}\text{e}$

8. $^{1}_{0}\text{n} + \ ^{10}_{5}\text{B} \longrightarrow \underline{\hspace{1.5cm}} + \ ^{4}_{2}\text{He}$

CONCEPTUAL PHYSICS

Nuclear Fission and Fusion

1. Complete the table for a chain reaction in which two neutrons from each step individually cause a new reaction.

EVENT	1	2	3	4	5	6	7
NO. OF REACTIONS	1	2	4				

2. Complete the table for a chain reaction where three neutrons from each reaction cause a new reaction.

EVENT	1	2	3	4	5	6	7
NO. OF REACTIONS	1	3	9				

3. Complete these beta reactions, which occur in a breeder reactor.

$$^{239}_{92}U \longrightarrow \underline{\hspace{1.5cm}} + ^{0}_{-1}e$$

$$^{239}_{93}Np \longrightarrow \underline{\hspace{1.5cm}} + ^{0}_{-1}e$$

4. Complete the following fission reactions.

$$^{1}_{0}n + ^{235}_{92}U \longrightarrow ^{143}_{54}Xe + ^{90}_{38}Sr + \underline{\hspace{1cm}} \left(^{1}_{0}n\right)$$

$$^{1}_{0}n + ^{235}_{92}U \longrightarrow ^{152}_{60}Nd + \underline{\hspace{1cm}} + 4\left(^{1}_{0}n\right)$$

$$^{1}_{0}n + ^{239}_{94}Pu \longrightarrow \underline{\hspace{1.5cm}} + ^{97}_{40}Zr + 2\left(^{1}_{0}n\right)$$

5. Complete the following fusion reactions.

$$^{2}_{1}H + ^{2}_{1}H \longrightarrow ^{3}_{2}He + \underline{\hspace{1.5cm}}$$

$$^{2}_{1}H + ^{3}_{1}H \longrightarrow ^{4}_{2}He + \underline{\hspace{1.5cm}}$$

KNOW NUKES!

CONCEPTUAL PHYSICS